**happy
people are
annoying**

happy people are annoying

Josh Peck

HarperOne
An Imprint of HarperCollins*Publishers*

Some names and identifying details in this book have been changed to protect the privacy of the individuals involved.

HarperCollins books may be purchased for educational, business, or sales promotional use. For information, please email the Special Markets Department at SPsales@harpercollins.com.

FIRST EDITION

Designed by Kyle O'Brien

Library of Congress Cataloging-in-Publication Data is available upon request.

ISBN 978-0-06-307361-6

22 23 24 25 26   LSC   10 9 8 7 6 5 4 3 2 1

For E.A.D.

Contents

Introduction
Happy People Are Annoying

You are an amalgamation of trauma; I hate to break it to you. There's a good chance that someone in the past five generations of your ancestral tree lived an incredibly unfair existence. So unfair in fact that their sole purpose was survival and the thought of living a good life didn't go much further than making sure they had enough to eat that day. Can you believe that? No bucket list? No vision boards?

I didn't stand a chance at being normal, and I'm guessing if you picked up a book with a sassy title like this one, you didn't either. My birth alone was fraught with an innumerable amount of fuckery (more on that in chapter 1). However, because the instinct to procreate is so deeply embedded in our brain, because the best part of having kids is making 'em, our ancestors threw caution to the wind, along with any and all forms of contraception available at the time, and said, "Screw it! Let's do it!" They could have spared us this odd experiment that is existence, but they didn't and thank God for tequila, lest many of us would have remained but sparkles in our parents' eyes.

We're all playing catch-up. From the moment we're born we're the beneficiaries of millennia of struggle. We've inherited the best and worst of everyone who came before us, we had no say in the matter. We didn't elect to be born, pick our parents, our circumstances, or our environment. People we've never met, people we've never even thought about, all had a hand in the hand we were dealt and it's our job, as far as I can tell, to correct the bad behavior of everyone who came before us.

I mean, what's there not to be happy about?

1

Sex and Deli

Here's what I know. My father was a semihandsome, older, curly-haired man who owned an apartment in Manhattan and a home in the country, which, anyone who grew up in New York City knows, is the sign of someone with disposable income and their shit together. In the dog days of summer, there is nothing more coveted than a friend with a country home and an open invitation, so that you may escape the smell of hot trash and traffic, if just for the weekend. My father had it all, a thriving business, a wife and kids, and at sixty-two, the makings of what should have been a triumphant victory march toward convalescence.

Until he knocked up my mom, that is.

Getting pregnant is both easier and harder than we think. As teens, we're conditioned to believe that a mere glance could get someone pregnant, that the safest course of action is to seal oneself inside a giant condom indefinitely, until we have permission from God, our parents, and the president to procreate. As we get older, of course, we're met with the reality that procreating can be quite difficult for some people, and an entire billion-dollar industry is devoted to those for whom getting pregnant is challenging. And while people are having kids success-fully later and later these days, there is still the assump-tion that after forty you might just want to adopt.

My mom was forty-two. She had always wanted kids, but biology being the cruel arbiter it is had decided she had missed her sell-by date. "Want" is one thing. Being a fit candidate to spawn new life is another. And the sands of time were not moving in her favor. It was a dream she'd given up on, an agreement one makes when they've crossed that invisible line that says, "I suppose I'll just have to sleep in, every day, forever."

So *how*, you may ask, how did the egg of a forty-two-year-old woman and the seed of a sixty-two-year-old man, having hooked up only once (or so she tells me and also, gross), intermingle to produce the icon writing here before you? HOW did this miraculous bit of birthing oc-cur, second only to the immaculate conception of Jesus himself? The answer, simply, is deli. It must be deli.

The Carnegie Deli was a New York landmark for more than seventy-nine years. Opened in 1929, it served its loyal customers oversize portions of pastrami and corned beef slathered in Russian dressing, and sometime in February of 1986 it served my mother and father a late-night post-coital feast. (I hate that sentence a lot.) And while yes, it's reasonable to think that deli, having no known reproductive qualities, had nothing to do with the miracle of birth that occurred that night, I still like to think that the sodium of the pickles, or the bubbles of the cream soda, were somewhat responsible for pushing the puck past the goalie.

My mom and dad knew each other, kind of. Before the deli, they were acquaintances, business colleagues, the kind of people who meet twice a year for lunch and at the end say "we should do this more often" but never do. They weren't close enough to share a sandwich, let alone a baby, and I'm sure when my father found out my mom was pregnant, similar thoughts came crashing through his philandering head. Now, I'm not one for slander, and while I've not named this mysterious man I call Dad, I'll give him the benefit of the doubt when he told my mom he was "separated" from his wife the night I was conceived. And hasn't he paid his karmic debt anyway? I mean, gosh, nothing gets in the way of a well-intentioned affair like impregnating a person whose middle name you don't know.

I don't know a lot about my dad but I do know a lot about being a man, and while I can only speak for myself, I know what it feels like to be blinded by the thrill of a romantic interlude. I also know the feeling you get once it's over, realizing that perhaps there was more to be considered before engaging in such a consequential act. All that to say, I'm sure my dad was just trying to get some. And get some he did, some illegitimate son, that is. Sure, it was irresponsible of him to disregard the realities of a possible pregnancy, but thank God he did! Thanks for throwing caution to the wind, Dad, happy to be here!

So, you're probably asking yourself, *Who does this?* Who sleeps with a man who is supposedly separated, after she was summoned to his high-rise apartment for some "business advice" (oh, Mom), gets pregnant, and decides to keep the kid, knowing full well she might have to do this alone. That woman is Barbara Peck, and she's my mother.

My mom is an enigma. A once-in-a-generation type of person, a tigress, an empath, a counterculture Jewish priestess who has been sticking her middle finger up to societal norms since she was a kid. Simply put, she gives very few fucks, and until I was born, made a habit of breaking convention in how she worked, lived, and loved. It was not an odd occurrence for her to jump in a car, drive the twelve-hundred-mile trip to Florida, cut hair on the beach all summer for pocket money, or get fired from being a waitress for sitting down with customers and picking food off their plates. One of my favorite stories is when she opened up an employment agency at twenty-six, only to be held up by robbers a few weeks into starting the business. When I asked if she was scared she replied, "Scared? No, I mean no one likes getting tied up, but I tried to offer the guys a job, seemed silly that they would rob an employment agency, they should have just filled out an application." That's my mom. Fearless.

So there she stood, pregnant, unmarried, in her early forties, and ready for whatever came next. It shouldn't have happened, the odds were not in her favor, so the fact that she was pregnant seemed like a cosmic confluence of events.

My father, on the other hand, was, let's just say, less excited about this whole cosmic confluence. Here's the thing, I don't blame him for not wanting to be in my life. "Majority rules" someone once said to me when I told them that I didn't know my dad. It took me a minute to digest what that meant. They went on to say, "I mean, ya know, he had a wife and three kids who were already grown, a whole other life. So when given the choice between them or you and your mom, I guess majority rules." Simple. Brutal. True?

My mom did a really good job of obfuscating the reality of my dad and what she went through after she found out she was pregnant. Maybe "obfuscate" is the wrong word, perhaps "omit" is better. At a young age she told me the good things about him, that he was successful, a charming businessman, a handsome raconteur, you might say (don't worry, I don't know what "raconteur" means either). And I believed her. I walked around day care thinking, *There is some incredible guy out there who is a real bespoke-type gentleman, a man about town, a socialite.* A Jewish James Bond strolling the streets of Manhattan in a Brooks Brothers suit and an eight hundred credit score. Sure, he wants nothing to do with me, but other than that, he seems sterling!

Later, as I got older and was able to handle it, Mom started coloring in the story for me. The stories of him refusing to meet with her when she told him she was pregnant, requesting she go get a paternity test and after receiving the results, accusing her and the doctor of being in cahoots. Later he demanded she get a paternity test with *his* doctor, and when she showed up expecting to see my dad there, the doctor told her to please leave. She'd called his bluff—and that was it. Finally, out of options, he just kinda . . . went away. He pretty much disappeared in plain sight. He didn't go into witness protection, he just acted as though none of it was happening, he returned back to his fantastic life, leaving my mom in a precarious position.

A surprise is a birthday party, a mistake is a DUI. A surprise is a winning lotto ticket, a mistake is getting caught smuggling drugs at the airport. They're two very different things, and yet somehow, me being born can be categorized as both. It's interesting to be able to assign different words to the same thing and have them both be true.

My mom had a brother who died of leukemia when he was ten. Sixteen and heartbroken, she said the only thing that mended that broken heart was twenty-six years later, when she had me. I mean, with that level of Hallmarkian platitude, it's no wonder she was able to withstand the hardships of single motherhood from jump. She spent the next nine months saving what she could, setting up a nursery in her apartment, throwing herself a baby shower, and eating hot croissants from the French bakery around the corner from her house, which explains my early-onset high cholesterol. For her, surprise!

For Dad, mistake. I was an accident, a blemish. He rolled the dice and they came up double holy shit. He was sixty-two, this wasn't a guy who was figuring his life out, sharing some prewar apartment in Williamsburg with three other roommates. This was an established dude, someone who had spent most of his life probably having successful affairs. Or maybe not! But either way, he was *not* going to shake up his world by doing the right thing, it was just never going to happen. Majority rules, remember? So when my mom asked him to contribute, to at least help financially if not physically with the whole rearing of a human being thing, one he donated twenty-three chromosomes to, he passed. A hard no. Come on, Dad. . . . Do you mind if I call you Dad?

Well, you all know how these things go, nine months and copious amounts of hot croissants later, there I was, born at New York Hospital, a solid thirteen pounds, eight ounces. Just kidding. I was a svelte seven pounds, thirteen ounces and have been actively working to get back to my birth weight ever since. All the nurses couldn't stop talking about how lean I looked in a onesie, trust me. In a fit of alchemy, my mom gave birth to The Man in her life, me. I was her son first but her life partner second, and we were about to muddle through this thing together, for better or worse, in sickness and in health, till death do us part.

Don't let the incestuous undertones of that last statement fool you, it's not like that. Look, when you're a single mom and an only child, the dynamic is one of pilot and co-pilot. It has to be, especially when you're struggling, which is most of the time for a parent doing it on their own. My friends who grew up in traditional family structures seemed to be part of a closed corporation. They and their siblings were employees, some with seniority, of course, but all around the same pay scale. Then there were their parents, upper management, who barked out orders over the radio. My mom and I were more like a scrappy start-up, juking and jiving just to stay afloat. Sometimes the CEO would have to sweep the floors and other times the assistant would get to pitch the big investors.

It was shortly after I was born that my father, in a crisis of conscience, decided to do the right things, acknowledge my existence and help financially to oversee my life, if only from afar. Just kidding. My mom took him to court.

She asked her best friend, Jeff, to represent her. As far as I know Jeff has never practiced family law but definitely went to law school. Shout out Jeff. The three of us headed one cold morning in November to the New York County Supreme Court. There she stood on the steps of the courthouse, her lawyer on one side, her baby on the other, waiting to beg a judge to force my dad to do the right thing. I mean is this not the stuff of fairy tales or what?!

My dad showed up with his lawyer, cold, clinical, and ready to clear up this whole "mess." I can't imagine what it was like for my mom to stand there with her new baby and look at this disappointing man she shared deli with only a few months prior. Before they made it to the judge, my father's lawyer asked for a sidebar with my mom's attorney, and by the time it was over, they'd agreed on a one-time payment. An asshole tax. My mom knew he didn't want to be involved and certainly she didn't want to chase him for child support for the next eighteen years, so yeah, she took the money, which was probably the equivalent of three or four years of child support, and sent him on his way. Clearly, my dad wanted no record of this transaction, and in hindsight, she probably should've fought for the child support, but my mom's always been more of a lump sum kind of gal.

I've asked my mom a lot about the day she took my dad to court. I've always been slightly in awe of how it all went down, especially my dad's ability to just disconnect. "Didn't he cry? Beg for forgiveness?! Look at you deeply in the eyes and say, in another life, you and me, kid, we could've had it all? Something?!" My mom replied, "After we were done, he looked at you sleeping in your stroller, touched his heart, and walked off. That was it."

Hmm, now, I don't know if that's true or not. Not that I think my mom is lying to me, it's just that memory is a funny thing, and sometimes we put a halo of decency around situations, especially when we're trying to make our kids feel like the world isn't unjust. But we know it is, the world is unjust, this is not new, some of us are just introduced to it sooner than others. From what I can tell, the pieces I've put together, I think he just wrote a check and left.

That money, like most money in our life, lasted until it didn't, and with the final dollar went the last connection we had to him. When I was five, my mom sent him a letter and a picture of me that I'm sure never arrived because who wouldn't reach out to an estranged lover after catching a glimpse of such a fetching five-year-old? Maybe he saw the writing on the wall, that I was destined to be a chubby child star and wanted no part of it, or maybe at seventy he didn't want to summon the herculean amount of courage it would have taken to tell his family about me. Maybe he was just scared. Either way, I gotta hand it to the guy, once he made a decision, he sure did stick to it. I like to think I inherited that quality from him, just in a less evil way, like the kid of a drug dealer who never understood why he was so good at math.

I've thought about him a lot throughout my life. Like pain for a phantom limb, absent fathers have a really cute way of invading your thoughts. Father's Day? Not my favorite. Even those sneaky questions at the doctor's office. Father's health history? Um, bad at commitment but with a formidable libido? Oh, and there's always the fun moment of having to deliver lines to an actor playing my father in a TV show or a movie. I always secretly worry I'm not doing it right, that the words "Hey, Dad" will come out funny, like a foreign language. Might just be lack of talent, but I'll blame it on the old man.

It's worth exploring my mom's culpability in all this. I mean, it takes two to tango, isn't that why it's a saying? And there are two sides to every story, so yeah, I'm sure there're things she could have done differently. She didn't have to get pregnant and she certainly didn't have to keep it. God knows there were enough signs along the road glaring, STOP, HAZARD, THE DUDE'S MARRIED, HE LITERALLY DOESN'T EVEN WANT TO PAY FOR A SANDWICH. It's not like she was under the impression my dad was going to stick around, leave his family, and move us to Long Island so I could play lacrosse and develop a really unfortunate accent.

The writing was on the wall: she was signing up for the potential of a really tough life.

When I was six, My mom and I went to file for welfare after, let's just call it, a financially challenging few months. A homely woman behind an incredibly thick piece of glass responded, "We'll need to contact the boy's father before we're able to give any type of assistance."

My mom weighed her options, looked down at this kid, this new appendage she created, and told them to forget it. The idea of someone from local government calling my father, looking for him to put his hand in his pocket, and the emotional fallout that could result just wasn't worth it. All for some EBT and food stamps? No thanks. She got us into this and she'd get us out of it, with or without the help of the State of New York.

Here's what I know, she showed up. For the first nine months I mean I was a literal interloper, feeding off her nutrients, but every day since then and for my entire life she's shown up for me. A ship is safe in the harbor but that ain't what ships are made for. So I'm less interested in how you flex your yacht and more interested in how you fare in the rough seas. Because calm seas never made a skilled sailor! Where the fuck am I getting all these maritime references from?! And sure, my mom might have paddled out in bad weather but she never let us sink. She battened down the hatches when it stormed and raised the sails when the wind blew.

She's the captain of our ship, and she always got us home.

2

Too Fat for Commercials

When I was ten years old, I overheard my mom having a heated conversation with my agent—I won't mention her name but if you're reading this, you were probably right. Also though, I was ten, so I think that still makes you a bad person.

Mom: I just don't understand why Josh doesn't have more auditions.

Agent: I don't know what to tell you, Barbara.

Mom: So many of his friends are auditioning twice a week. We're only going out once or twice a month.

Agent: I really don't know what to tell you.

Mom: Well, can you offer any advice?

Agent: Yes. Tell Josh to lose fifty pounds and dye his hair blond. Oreo is not going to have a fat kid in their commercial. It's just never gonna happen.

Brutal.

In her defense, she was right. I mean there's just no way a bunch of Nabisco executives were sitting around a conference room spitballing ideas on how to empower gigantic pre-teens. No ad exec wants to even hint at the fact that many of these snack foods are caloric grenades on kids' metabolisms. Still, growing up, this conversation and others had an effect. Here's another one.

> **Pediatrician:** He's very overweight. This is dangerous.
> I think we need to put him on a low-carb, low-sugar diet
> immediately.
> **Mom:** Right. I understand. But he is eight.
> **Pediatrician:** That may be true, Ms. Peck, but he's got
> the bloodwork of a fifty-year- old.
> **Mom:** Isn't there a chance that as he grows taller, he'll
> even out?
> **Pediatrician:** That depends. Anyone in your family
> six-eight?

Dr. Blumenfeld, great guy, shout out Dr. Blumenfeld. Actually, shout out every pediatrician I had who had tried to put a twelve-year-old on cholesterol medication before their bar mitzvah. Also, why did no one have these conversations without me present? I guess the truth is, for every conversation I did hear, there were probably two more I didn't. I'm sure there were plenty of opinions being tossed in my mom's direction, of how she could best intervene in my Pop-Tart habit.

"Send him to a fat camp!" I heard that a lot. "I sent Jeremy there last summer and when he got home, I barely recognized him!" Jewish mothers love to send their kids off to camp to heal them from the food issues they implanted themselves when they wouldn't excuse us before we finished our plates. And while I like tick bites and canoeing as much as the next kid, I'm not sure expensive sleep-away camp was going to get in the way of me and my pesky habit.

Actually, it wasn't a habit. It was love, my first love.

We all have a memory that comes to mind when we think about childhood. For some it's a Rockwellian scene of playing outside as the sun dips below the horizon. For my wife, it was her grandfather picking her and her siblings up after dinner and taking them for ice cream. I love imagining her breathing in the crisp, Sacramento air as she took a bite of her Raspberry Ribbon. On second thought, maybe I just like the ice cream, which would totally explain this next sentence.

For me, when I think of childhood, the singular, powerful, and all-consuming memory that comes to mind is being fat. That's my anchor. It's like a bug on the lens. No matter how beautiful the background, all you're thinking is, *Get that bug off the damn lens!* I have good memories from childhood too, of course, I grew up with a deep awareness that I was loved, decent, cared for, and blah blah blah, but FAT, very very fat. How fat?

I was 297 pounds. This is beyond big-boned. I would've needed to be six-ten and from Samoa for this weight to sit correctly on my frame. This was morbidly obese, this was get-your-stomach-cut-out, weight-loss-surgery-level fat. Out-of-breath-in-the-shower, break-a-chair, seat-belt-extender, "God, why doesn't he just control himself" fat.

I don't want it to sound like I'm speaking in hyperbole here or making fun of myself, everything I just said is absolutely true. Some people might say, "Hey, I'm a bigger dude and I carry it just fine." Good for you, go write a book about it. I, however, did not look like I played offensive line for Alabama, I looked like a walking time bomb, and if I'm going to make a statement such as "My one memory of childhood is being fat" I just want to make sure you understand the magnitude.

"Faking good" is a neuropsychological term for adopting a favorable behavior you believe will serve your interests. There are many ways you can present a different picture from your inner reality . . . but not when you're overweight. It walks in the room before you do, you can't tuck it away.

Growing up, there was an energy surrounding food in my house. It was the central focus. The main event. You're going to a Yankee game? GREAT, you'll have a hot dog. It's a Jewish holiday? GREAT, we'll have brisket.

We're going out? GREAT, we'll grab pizza. Staying in?

GREAT, let's order Chinese. Food was it. Weddings were good because there were pigs and blankets on little trays, being passed around by waiters who turned a blind eye to the fact that I had been camped out by the kitchen door, waiting for the next batch to come out. Movies? Well, that was the mecca because that's where popcorn lived.

I'll never forget when my friend comedian Lisa Lampanelli blew my mind with this life hack: "Ya know what the fat girl move is at the movies, right? You get your big bag of popcorn and then you hook up a straw to the butter dispenser and shove that thing all the way down your bag. This way, you get butter on every layer of the popcorn, instead of just the top." Those are some high-level big-people moves.

Growing up, I had an almost immediate abnormal relationship with food. I would observe friends who would freely pop open a bag of fruit snacks and not obsess over the other six in the cabinet. Kids who when their parents washed their clothes didn't have melted chocolate bars in their pocket. I knew I was different but it also wasn't an issue yet; all kids like candy, most kids have baby weight, I was a typical baby! We LOVE being typical.

Unfortunately, while all kids might *like* candy, while all kids might look forward to an ice cream truck or a pizza party. I LOVED it. I obsessed over it, enough to lie, cheat, and steal just to get my fix. If that meant sneaking into your family's snack drawer when I came over, like an addict rummaging through a stranger's medicine cabinet? So be it.

This behavior, as far as I can tell, was the by-product of two distinct things. First, I liked the way delicious things made me feel, full stop. I didn't know it at the time obviously but I was definitely medicating something deep within. I just didn't eat junk food like other kids, I was voracious, I couldn't get enough, I thought there was a finite amount of fruit snacks in the world and it was incumbent on me to get my fair share. Even if that meant having to barter with you at lunch with a twenty-dollar bill I'd found in the boys' bathroom hours earlier. Imagine my six-year-old chagrin when I got pulled into the principal's office and heard, "Jordan tells us you gave him twenty dollars for his Zebra Cakes?"

Jordan the Rat. Why do you hate money, Jordan?!

The second Miracle-Gro for the seedlings of my obsession was that we didn't have those good foods at home. My mom has always had a warped relationship with food, literally getting on or off a diet my entire life. From ages five to eight, I watched her weight constantly fluctuate. For most of my life she has brought a purse-size scale with her wherever she goes, so that she can weigh and measure everything she eats. It's normal to me now, I actually get worried when I don't see the scale, but it does invite some unsolicited questions from the waitstaff at Cheesecake Factory. Oh, I'm sorry. I thought I was here for the brown bread and mid-century

Tuscan aesthetic, not an interrogation! And lest we forget I was conceived during deli or literally minutes before.

Scales for weighing your food, scales for weighing your body, diet foods, diet snacks, weight-loss support groups, medical weight-loss programs, weight-loss drugs, and plus-size clothing stores, that was my normal.

Except for the few times a year she went off her diet and the wheels REALLY came off. I was never on a diet growing up, not for more than twenty-four hours anyway, but still I had to hide my really damaging eating from my mom. Sneaking away to the corner store, trading with kids at school, the friends' house snack closet capers as I mentioned, there was just a lot of sneaking going on; it was Ocean's Eleven at my house. My mom had to hide from me too, the moments when she went off her diet and didn't want the world to know we were a family of thieves. But there were those rare times when she really wanted to do some damage and didn't care who knew it, then we would partner up—there wasn't a pizza joint, Chinese restaurant, or deli in New York that was safe. We'd hit the local drugstore on the way home and buy three or four bags each of whatever cookie or candy combo screamed our name and retreat to our rooms so we could eat in peace. It didn't seem odd, it seemed fun. I could finally eat how I wanted to.

That was what food was like in my house, that was my introduction. Food was something to be celebrated and something to be hidden, it was to be ruthlessly controlled, weighed, and measured or completely overindulged in, it was good and evil. Food was powerful, the focal point, something to do when there was nothing to do. It made you fat, and fat was bad because people teased you, but it was also good, just not too much, "just have one, Josh, like your friends, don't you have self-control?" Food was a menacing force to the Pecks, I watched it since I could form memories. It terrorized my mom and I could see, even through the lens of childhood, that it was already terrorizing me.

Being overweight, especially in the nineties before the antibullying, body-positivity era of today, invited a lot of commentary and critique. I want to say something here before I go any further, today IS better. I don't mean to make light of body positivity, it's important and anyone who today feels more comfortable in their skin than they did when the only standard of beauty was a supermodel, I applaud you. For too long we walked around seeing beautiful people in all shapes and sizes that literally had no representation and today it's drastically better. But being overweight when I was overweight was different. We didn't have the same guardrails we have in place today, it was open season on anyone who looked different, and the products of that were people like me walking around pretty uncomfortable.

Adults who cared about me always commented on my weight with no thought of how it might make me feel.

Unsolicited advice would come in the form of "He needs more sports!" or "He'll grow out of it!" or "It's soda, soda is a goddamn killer for kids!" It was like people were screaming at me, "Be less handicapped!" It wasn't that I was too dumb to get it, if given the option to choose the thin or the chubby pill, I would've chopped up the skinny pill and mainlined it into whatever vein was closest. But I just wasn't equipped, the problem was rooted deeper than my ability to deal with it.

Imagine being a sensitive, powerless kid who develops this habit that brings them comfort and peace, a coping mechanism to keep the world and their feelings at bay, but at the same time distorts their body, inviting teasing and criticism, which wounds them, and the only salve they know to ease that pain is to eat more. Holy crap, that's a cycle. I remember the first time a kid called me a fat fuck at the JCC. That's the Jewish Community Center, shout out Jews and our community centers. I was eight years old at an after-school program and the kid just hit me with it, straight to the chest, Tupac-style. "Hey, you fat fuck." Until that point I had sort of operated with impunity, I knew I was bigger than the other kids but was unbothered by it until that comment, that comment was the first that wounded. It pierced my armor, waking me up to the idea that life might be tough looking like this. And at the JCC of all places, we could've fought but someone would've got their yarmulke knocked off.

I'm going to jump ahead now because I'd just be repeating myself. More eating, more teasing, more failed diet attempts, more biannual binge fests with Mom. A lot of people grew up overweight and I imagine their experience was similar, but here's where mine was different. As I got a little older, I did what any self-respecting, overweight kid deeply uncomfortable with their appearance and navigating the social battlefield of puberty would do. I decided to be on television.

The beautiful by-product of my appearance, the silver lining to it all, was that I had developed a finely tuned sense of humor. Like a consolation prize, the world said, "You're going to be massively overweight, so here, be funny." If you're a tall kid, someone should hand you a basketball as soon as possible, there's no excuse to be over six-six and not have a jump shot. Similarly, if you're fat, it helps to be funny.

If I could make you laugh then perhaps you wouldn't make fun of me. In fact, if I could make you laugh, perhaps I could control the entire conversation or even the entire energy of the room. Comedy is like a superpower you can employ whenever you want. I'm sure it's primordial, the effect it has on people, it calms the tribe, distracting people from the worries of their lives. I'd had a master class in it my whole life watching my mother do it—she developed her comedic skills I'm sure for similar reasons. She was overweight, but it didn't matter, she'd walk into a room and take it over. The entertainment is here so shut up or get run over. I learned it all from her. She's seventy-seven now and still kills with a one-liner.

"The reason why people are funny is usually not funny at all."

I don't know where that quote's from but it fits. I had acquired a set of skills to help me navigate the world around me. I became a natural choice for school plays, after-school theater programs, whatever—because my life was one big performance anyway, a highly crafted show to keep people's eyes where I wanted them to go. I also really liked performing. Of course, eventually, I'd have to face this aversion to actually being myself instead of this character I had created, but that would come so much later. Right now? It was time to be funny on the big stage, show business responds well to such tools, and God bless Hollywood for keeping the emotionally handicapped gainfully employed since the days of silent movies.

You'll find this out in the next chapter, but when I was fifteen and probably the biggest I'd ever been, I had my own television show with my name in it. Not one that I could watch, of course, I was too embarrassed to enjoy the reality of myself onscreen, but a show nonetheless! I was getting to do this thing that I loved, on the highest level possible. But I was also introducing myself to the world as someone I knew I didn't want to be.

I was living my dream, I was just doing it in the wrong body.

I'll never forget when the costume designer for the show took mercy on me after seeing me pull on my wardrobe for the hundredth time. With every tug I must've thought that somehow the fabric would become more flattering. She brought me into her office and said, "Hey, I want to try something, put this on." She handed me what looked like a tank top but it was skin-colored and about two sizes too small. I thought, *What is this, some cruel joke? I should just fold myself into this sausage casing for your amusement? This woman is a chubby chaser, I know it!* Against my better judgment, though, I put the shirt on and instantly understood its purpose. This angel of a costume designer had built me homemade SPANX.

That's right, ladies and gentlemen, a man girdle, a Lycra bodysuit that smoothed out every roll and every bulge. Wearing this magical tunic, I no longer resembled a gigantic muffin and now looked more like an over-stuffed bag of bread. It wasn't perfect, but it was better and I felt better. So I wore it, every day, for five years.

I was wearing SPANX Men's, a corset, on national television, at 290 pounds, in five million homes, every Sunday night. Hollywood is glamorous as fuck.

So that's where I was at sixteen. I was at a crossroads. I was fat, famous, and freaking out. I didn't like the way I looked but how I looked was part of what got me here. "But Josh, maybe you would've been funny regardless of how you looked." When Mike Tyson was asked how he became such a good boxer, he replied, "I grew up in

Brownsville." As if to say, having an affinity for combat is a natural result of growing up in such a violent place. Nurture matters, circumstance matters, and all the events in my life had conspired to bring me to this point.

But what if I wanted to let it go? Should I? Could I? Would it be foolish to try to lose weight now that I was the funny fat guy?

I realized I was part of a legacy. Chris Farley, John Belushi, they weren't any more or less talented because they were overweight, but the audience grew to love them this way. There's something about a funny fat guy that puts people at ease, like the wrapper of your favorite candy bar, "Ahhhh I know what this is, I love what this is." Farley and Belushi are both dead by the way. Did I dare try to do it all? Do what I love *and* like the way I looked? Isn't that privilege reserved for happy people?

I had to decide, stick with what works? Or go for the life I wanted? Should I try for happy?

3

The Laughing Jew Welcome Committee

I was eight years old at a Jewish holiday dinner. Jews love to come together and share in the overall theme of Judaism, which is, "They tried to kill us, we lived, let's eat." I was sitting there, drunk on carbs, watching the adults interact, when I got an impulse to tell a joke I'd overheard my mom tell weeks before. It was slightly dirty, not obscene but colorful and certainly not something an eight-year-old should tell when celebrating his people's exodus from Egypt. I waited for my opening, for the conversation to break, and then I let it fly. Full commitment.

So much in my life could have been different had they not laughed. I could be an accountant in Dallas right now. I could be an attorney in Florida. I could be a Bitcoin miner in Norway. But I'm none of those things. I'm none of those things because they laughed, they laughed their asses off.

If meditation is like golf for the brain, then comedy is the ultimate action sport. It's utterly ballistic. You can't have a plan, you have to adjust to the way the ball bounces and decide in a millisecond how much topspin you want to put on it.

Imagine shifting the energy of an entire room when you were supposed to be at the kids' table, becoming the boy king in a matter of seconds. People can be too much of a lot of things—too smart, too nosy, too gullible—but you're never too funny. No one ever said, "Ya know that Rick is great but when I'm around him I laugh TOO much." It doesn't happen. It's as close to a magic trick as you can get because when it's good, really good, people are left wondering how you did it, and if you can do it again. There's a sense of wonderment. Comedy has made people rich, given stays of execution, and most importantly, made the ugly attractive for millennia.

That table of laughing Jews was all I needed, they were the welcome committee to my life's work.

The arts were revered in my home growing up. My mom and I had a regular habit of sneaking into Broadway shows during intermission, they would leave the theater doors open so people could smoke, which was perfect because we could just slip in and grab empty seats. Sure we missed the first half, but you couldn't beat the price. We'd spend weekends strolling the massive halls of the Metropolitan Museum of Art (partly because it was free), sing our hearts out on road trips down to Florida, and travel all through the tri-state area to watch her favorite jazz singers and cabaret acts. Musical theater nerds, you get the picture.

By now you might be catching on to a theme, one of a lack of money. Being broke wasn't a new concept for my mom and me, we tended to vacillate between periods of maybe middle class and almost poverty. She was a single mom with a high school education doing the best she could, sometimes that meant new video games and cheap vacations, other times it meant sharing a slice of pizza for dinner. It was what it was.

This level of financial volatility gave way to some pretty interesting situations. I was eight and we had just returned to New York from Florida, where we had been living for the past few years, partly because my grandmother was there and partly because it's easier to have less money in Florida. Shout out Florida and their lack of state income tax. We always made it back to New York, though, no matter where we went because at her core, I think my mom wanted us to be citizens of the greatest city in the world. The hustle, the culture, the diversity, she wanted to make sure her kid grew up in the middle of that, even if we couldn't afford it.

So there we were, back in our hometown, in a month-to-month studio apartment we couldn't afford, trading between the bed and the couch, wondering what the hell we were going to do. This was not uncommon for the Pecks. We were struggling, but it wasn't unbearable. Not for me

at least. Mom did a good job of making it all feel temporary, like "Yes this sucks, and yes the moving company
just sold all our possessions because we couldn't afford to
pay them, but this pizza is good and the TV works so let's
enjoy until Mom figures it out."

And she always did figure it out. So that's where we were.
Capsized in Manhattan, Mom spending her days looking
for work and me spending my days with my best friend.

Television.

Throughout my life, television has been my best friend,
my babysitter, my teacher, and, most importantly, my escape. I left it on to feel like someone was there, I fell asleep
to it, so the room never got dark. I watched Gene Wilder
in *Willy Wonka* and forgot I was broke. I watched *Sleepless
in Seattle* and wished Tom Hanks was my dad. I watched
Robin Williams in *Mrs. Doubtfire* and thought, *This is
the greatest thing I've ever seen.* Ace Ventura, Billy Madison, The Fresh Prince, they were all my closest confidants,
and becoming an actor felt as close to physically jumping
through the screen as I could get. I felt indebted to television, like working for the hospital that cured your cancer.

Television was my escape, my circumstance, my eight-
year-old worries stood no chance against Friday nights on
ABC or Saturday morning cartoons. I was a walking *TV
Guide*, I knew all the shows on every channel except for
Home and Garden because we neither had a home nor a
garden.

When hipster friends of mine talk about getting rid of their cable subscription or even worse, their television, I think, *Are you out of your Carhartt-wearing mind? What are you supposed to do with yourself? By the way, we all know you're watching Netflix on your laptop, so who are you kidding?* My son watches ALL THE TV, all of it. Not an obscene amount, we sprinkle it throughout the day, but let me tell you, at eighteen months the kid knew his ABCs and could count to thirty—pretty sure that was Elmo, not me. He eats chia seeds and can talk about his feelings too, just like the offspring of any proper millennial, but I'm just saying, TV, man, it's powerful.

I was obsessed with television and, much like food, when I like something, I overdo it. In this case, though, my obsession was an asset. I could watch the same movie or television show seventy-five times and be enthralled each time. Malcolm Gladwell says it takes ten thousand hours to get good at anything, well, these were my hours. I didn't know that's what I was doing at the time, I thought every kid consumes an inordinate amount of television, but through osmosis I was absorbing rhythms, cadence, the lyricism of performance. I was memorizing delivery, observing the way the actors moved, the way the audience reacted to those movements.

My favorites were sitcoms, probably because they portrayed families I wished I was a part of and because they had a live studio audience, so you knew what got the laugh. The comedian Colin Quinn said, "Comedy is the closest thing to justice because you get a laugh or you don't, there's no wondering whether it worked or not. It's fair." For a kid searching for a merit-based form of validation, this seemed like an effective route.

Comedy has a musicality to it, a rhythm, and while I couldn't yet understand why something was funny, I could *hear* it. I knew what funny sounded like, so like any great artist, I didn't borrow, I stole. I'd repeat bits I heard on TV to anyone who would listen. I'd perform at whatever afterschool program or holiday dinner was available. I couldn't take my act on the road so I'd do it at the supermarket, the doctor's office, wherever, always in search of a reaction, which should probably be the title of this book.

So my home life being what it was, mixed with my natural girth and heft pushing me to develop a sense of humor, along with me watching television like it was game tape all day, made me ready to go. I'd quickly conquered the school talent shows and Jewish holidays, it was time to go pro. I knew there was opportunity out there. I mean, I watched Kenan and Kel, Zach Morris, and Stephanie Tanner every day, how'd they get there? How did Disney and Nickelodeon seem to have a never-ending rotation of talented tweens? How could I get on that list? Sure, I literally had no connections. But who needs connections when you're chubby and ambitious? That's probably how I found myself at eight, scanning the pages of *Backstage* magazine, looking for a job like I'd just graduated from a state school with a communications degree.

Backstage was the preeminent magazine for actors, packed with endless articles about what's going on in the acting universe, gossip from Hollywood, and a section of classifieds in the back where agents and managers would advertise. I don't know how this magazine wound up in my possession, how it made its way into my eight-year-old hands, but it did, and that's how I found this ad shining like a beacon of hope. There it was, at three dollars a letter:

SID GOLD OF GOLDSTAR ENTERTAINMENT IS SEARCHING FOR YOUNG COMEDIANS TO REPRESENT. ALL AGES ARE WELCOME.

Whelp, last time I checked, I was all ages and this mysterious man, Sid Gold, seemed like the perfect candidate to become the Cus D'Amato to my Tyson. I begged my mom to make an appointment and she obliged, already noticing I had a voracious urge to change my circumstance, or maybe she thought it was cute that I wanted it so bad.

A few days later, we climbed the Victorian staircase of an old office building near Times Square and walked into the offices of Goldstar Entertainment. For me it was like walking into Google headquarters, when in hindsight it was more of a geriatric WeWork. Sid's lovely assistant/wife opened the door. "Oh, you're the little boy who called us."

"That's right, ma'am, I am the little boy and boy am I excited to be here."

Sid looked like he could have easily been one of my Jewish grandparents, in fact he might have been at that holiday dinner months earlier. Maybe that's why he agreed to represent me, or more likely because he saw the raw talent shooting out of my pores, or most likely because he said yes to everyone. "Ya think you can put together five minutes of stand-up? Because if ya can, I can get you stage time." I won't let ya down, Sid! Oh, by the way, do you want to be my dad? Just kidding, mostly!

I ran back to our apartment and started putting together an act, more stolen jokes from Mom, impressions of kids at school, observational baby, young Seinfeld vibes. I got booked for the following Sunday at Caroline's Comedy Club in midtown, it was a kids' comedy show at two in the afternoon, which is obviously a competitive timeslot for up-and-coming comedians in the city that never sleeps. I donned my best vest (it was kind of my look back then, Google it if you want to hurt your eyes) and set forth to put my comedic stake in the ground.

I killed. I absolutely crushed. They say the devil gives you the first ride for free, well this was that. I was possessed, I walked out there with all the confidence of a chubby eight-year-old with nothing to lose and I did just that, I didn't lose.

I started doing stand-up at every comedy club in New

York City. No more kid shows, these were adult rooms and they'd have to sneak me through the back door so the club wouldn't lose its liquor license. I'd go to school, come home, get a nap in, and then perform till eleven, everywhere and anywhere that would have me. Eventually, I realized how many comedians go onstage without material, they'd get up and just start doing crowd work, hoping that some divine comedic moment would be born in that second. I didn't have that luxury. I knew I had no frame of reference for crowd work, the audience probably wasn't into Pokémon like me, so I stuck to my set and became a mechanic at performing it. I took that routine to every club, church basement, and coffeehouse night after night.

A year or two went by and I was slowly becoming more successful. I'd upgraded agents—sorry, Sid, showbiz is brutal—I was starting to book commercials (none for Oreos), and my identity at school and with family and friends became more and more enmeshed with being the "actor kid." I did a few sketches on *Conan*, I did stand-up on *The Rosie O'Donnell Show*. I was sort of hitting this stride, the more I performed the better things got.

And then it all fell apart again.

Sticking with the theme of high highs and low lows in the Peck household, in 1998 my mom and I found ourselves broke. Again. Fuck. Fuck fuck fuck. I was twelve now and pissed. As I got older, the stress of being displaced started to weigh on me. There was always a sense of impending doom the months leading up to it—disaster was ahead. I'd notice my mom acting differently, incredibly stressed, tired, and then sort of manic as she went into hyperdrive trying to save us. Inevitably it always ended the same way, she'd tell me we had two weeks to pack up our stuff, and when those two weeks were up, we'd move back to Florida, or maybe California, or maybe just . . . just pack your stuff. She'd make it seem like it was on our terms, like we were choosing to live this nomadic life, right up until the moment we handed in our keys and had to figure out where we were sleeping that night.

This was July of 1998. For most, it was like any other New York City summer. Kids roamed the streets looking for open fire hydrants, Mister Softee trucks bombed down the avenues, and I was just trying to pass the time until school started.

I don't know when the light turns on in our consciousness, when the veil of adolescence falls and we clue into the real world around us, but for me, it was that summer. I remember suddenly and overwhelmingly feeling the stakes of my life for the first time—being broke, being powerless, and thinking, *I gotta do something about this.*

We all have moments like that, moments when we make a silent vow to ourselves and think, *I never want to feel this way again.* That was it for me. I didn't know how I was going to do it, acting was still just a hobby, I made very little money from it, how was I going to get us out of this?

At the moment, everything was technically okay. My grandmother had floated us some money and we had moved into a different crappy studio apartment. It didn't matter, that was the summer it was all going to change, I just had to figure out how.

"You don't really want to go to that school, do you?" my mom said as she fanned herself, trying to avoid the August heat. We had been in this crappy studio for two months now and I was eagerly awaiting school to start so I had something to do other than feel sorry for myself. I found it odd with ten days left of summer that she was asking whether I really wanted to go to that school. What did that even mean? It was middle school, not a bowling alley; I wasn't thrilled but I didn't mind. I had graduated fifth grade and was headed to the junior high school in my district, the one you go to whether you like it or not.

"You should audition for that Performing Arts School we heard about, seems like it could be good for you." And with that one sentence she changed the course of our lives. I mean, she was right, we were displaced, I didn't have a "district" anymore, why not?

A week later I auditioned and three days later I was walking the halls of the Professional Performing Arts School, a free public charter school in New York City, two blocks from the theater district. It welcomed all young performers in music, drama, and dance. Some alumni/alumnae include Alicia Keys, Jesse Eisenberg, Claire

Danes, and me, so as you can tell, I've listed our names in order of relevance.

The school was this melting pot of everything that's great about the arts. Every ethnicity, sexuality, and socioeconomic class was represented. There were dancers from the Alvin Ailey School, singers who would belt out songs through the hallways, and fifteen-year-old guys who held their boyfriend's hand during lunch.

Some of the teachers even did cartwheels at the end of semester. It was like Willy Wonka opened a high school.

I had always been such an oddity at my other school. That annoying kid who sucked at sports. The theater nerd. But here, I was one of many. Even at twelve, though, I was reminded by opinionated relatives that this "art school" was no way to make a living and it would behoove me to figure out a backup plan. By the way, I agreed with them. I didn't know any actors, especially kid actors who became adults with apartments.

But every day at this new school showed me that people didn't just survive as artists, they flourished. Some of my classmates, the ones on Broadway and TV shows, were making *real money*, nice-apartment money, own-a-car-in-New-York-City-so-you-don't-always-have-to-take-the-train money. I started to see a way out of my current situation, a way to make sure Mom and I were never poor again. Contrary to what my relatives thought, I *could* make money doing what I loved. Backup plan? What am I, a Boy Scout?!

Once I'd given my little twelve-year-old self permission to be an actor without apology, things got good fast. Over the next year, I threw myself into every comedy show, acting class, or open call that would have me, sitting in waiting rooms for three hours just to get the chance to audition. I soaked up everything school had to offer, taking drama, dance, and vocal classes, this was my renaissance, my rookie season.

My home life started to improve as well. My mom's business started doing well and we moved into a new apartment right by school. I was happy—truly happy—for the first time, maybe ever. I was popular at school, we seemed to have a little bit of money, and I was driven like I'd never been before, the blinders of my newfound passion helped tune out the world around me. I auditioned, auditioned, and auditioned, after school, during school, for anything and everything I could.

And then I booked something big.

Now, 1515 Broadway is a fifty-four-floor office building in the heart of Times Square. Inside lives the headquarters of Viacom, a billion-dollar, publicly traded, we-own-everything-style entertainment conglomerate with such subsidiaries as Paramount Studios, MTV, and a network that would soon become my employer for the next decade, Nickelodeon.

I was at 1515 every other day. The security guards knew me, so did the receptionists. Nickelodeon was always casting something and being twelve, chubby, and eager put me right in their wheelhouse. Whether it was a commercial, a showcase, or a TV show, I'd sign in, wait my turn, and grab something from the snack bar on my way out. Anything that kept me from going home a little longer, anything that brought me a little closer to what I loved.

Being in their faces month after month must have paid off because when Nickelodeon was holding auditions for their new movie *Snow Day* they knew who to call.

"He booked it," my agent said one Friday night in late January. I looked up from my chicken nuggets and thought, *I got it?* "What do you mean, he booked it?" my mom replied. "He got the movie," she said. "You leave for Canada on Wednesday for the next four months, hope you have your passports ready." There was a beat and then my mom said, "We don't have passports."

Snow Day was a Nickelodeon/Paramount movie starring Chevy Chase, Chris Elliott, Jean Smart, Iggy Pop, oh, and Josh Peck as its seventh lead. I'd booked a movie. A proper movie with a budget, trailers, and, wait for it— accommodations at the Sheraton Hotel in Calgary, Canada, for four glorious months. If being in a movie meant you got your own hotel room, one with room service and pay-per-view movies, I was ready to sign a Scientology-level life contract. It was heaven.

My school was used to actors leaving all the time to go work, and there was a tutor on set, so I was all good there. Mom bought something called a cellphone and ran her business out of a very Canadian pizza chain with the very American name of Boston Pizza. We were made for this! Remember we were a start-up, flexible, pliable, ready to pivot at a moment's notice, usually because shit hit the fan, but this was a good pivot! A positive pivot!

One particularly cold evening on set, my mom noticed me talking to some guy in a huge parka. I didn't know who he was but he had a great laugh, so I was hitting him with all my best material, material I had crafted over the past three years. As I headed toward the snack table, my mom asked, "You know that's the president of Nickelodeon, right? You should tell him you want to be on that show." I wondered what she meant until I realized, "Oh, you mean *that* show."

Growing up there was one television show that was my holy grail. It was called *All That*, and it was basically *Saturday Night Live* for kids. *All That* launched the careers of Kenan Thompson, Amanda Bynes, and Nick Cannon, and I was ready for it to launch mine except for one small hurdle, which was they wanted nothing to do with me. Over the past two years, I had auditioned to be a cast member on *All That* more than a dozen times, to rejection after rejection. We were at a stalemate, a null set.

So the next night, with the same confidence I had walking on that stand-up stage at eight years old, I told that president what I wanted most in the world. A father.

Kidding. I told him I should be on *All That*. The balls! The chutzpah! To tell the president of Nickelodeon, Albie Hecht, a maverick in the entertainment industry, someone who has gone on to be the president of multiple networks, that I, Josh Peck, president of nothing, should be on one of HIS shows.

Well, I guess it worked.

"Josh, it's Albie. I wanted to let you know that I'm flying you and your mom to California. You're gonna be on *The Amanda Show*, congrats." That was the phone call I received nine months later. It was like a triple-A ballplayer getting called up to the majors. "Can ya be here tonight? You're batting third in the lineup." I don't even know what the lesson is here. Shoot your shot?

I don't remember screaming, or crying, or having much of a reaction at all other than thinking, *What the eff is* The Amanda Show? *The Amanda Show* was a spin-off of *All That*, with Amanda Bynes starring in her own version of the same show. It was perfect, a huge hit for Nickelodeon. I couldn't believe it, this was the call I didn't know I had always been waiting for. I don't know what Albie saw in me, why he did this, but I owe him for it and I thank him every chance I get. We all need an Albie, someone with power who is willing to take a chance.

Seth Rogen talked about working with Judd Apatow early on in their careers.

After Judd's first film, *The Forty-Year-Old Virgin*, was

a hit at the box office, Judd called all his talented friends, Seth included, and said, "If you've got a script you've been sitting on, send it over. If we're ever going to get stuff made, it's now." Seth sent Judd the script for *Super Bad*, and well, we all know how that went.

I'd have my own experience with Judd Apatow later but right now, Albie was my Judd, he had the golden ticket and could bestow it upon anyone he pleased. Throughout life, you mostly meet other people on boats, but sometimes you meet the water. Albie was the water and when he rose, so did I. Another boating reference, Jesus, call me Commodore Peck over here.

So my mom and I packed up our '87 Mercedes and set off toward the Coast. We were leaving a lot behind, everyone we knew, our apartment, the school I loved, our identity as New Yorkers, but it didn't matter. This was the next step, the nomadic Pecks back at it again, never could stay anywhere too long. At least this time we had a legitimate reason to go. I'd been hired for twenty-four episodes of a major television show.

And I was never going to look back.

4

New Kid on the Lot

After spending five days traversing some of the finest interstates America has to offer, we landed in Los Angeles, the City of Angels, home of the Lakers, birthplace of the blues, pretty sure that last part isn't true. This was my time! I'd waited long enough, I'd done my time as a regular kid, but it was time to elevate, to level up, to start living the life of a successful actor. Hope ya like Lexuses, Mom, because we're going to be able to lease one!

There was just one problem, everyone hated me.

Okay, that's not completely true, they didn't hate me, they didn't KNOW me, and that was part of the problem. When I arrived on set, I was understandably the odd man out. "Who is this new guy?" The cast of *The Amanda Show* had already been together for the first season and I was crashing their party. Albie had pulled some presidential power moves to get me on the show. Unfortunately, the producers did not like that, and they proceeded to put me on ice for the first six episodes.

Which wasn't the worst thing. I mean I didn't love playing waiter number two in scenes, but I did need time to adjust. Everything was new, I was freshly thirteen, so adjusting to not only this new job but also this new life, three thousand miles from the old one, took a second. The truth is, only one person knew I could do this job and that was Albie. The producers certainly didn't know, and to be honest, neither did I. I knew I could perfectly re-create bits from TV shows, I knew I could do five minutes of stand-up. But this was the thing I'd been working for, the thing I'd dreamed of doing my entire life.

Now I just had to do it.

Luckily the silver lining of my heft came to my rescue, not for the first time, and I knew there was only one thing to do: get to work. I was used to walking into situations at a disadvantage, real or imagined. I thought people made a snap judgment about me because of the way I looked and it was incumbent on me to change their mind. So that's what I did. I became a student, watching every scene, every rehearsal I could, the way I did when I was eight staring at the television. Like in an apprenticeship, I mimicked the style of people such as Amanda Bynes, who, even though we were the same age, was a lifetime ahead of me in skill and ability. I knew how to be funny but I had to learn how to hone it, how to summon it under these new conditions. If I was going to be warming the bench, I'd study every second of the game instead of cursing the coach for not putting me in.

When I wasn't watching scenes or combing over the snack table, I'd spend time hanging out with the writers—doing bits and looking for father figures. Through this, day by day, they started to learn my voice. Suddenly I wasn't playing "Prickly Barista." I was playing characters I could do, like an idiot Mafioso or a panicked Boy Scout. Characters that required the kind of broad, loud, commanding comedic style I'd perfected.

There was another actor on the show, Drake Bell, whom I got matched up with a lot. We were great together, an undeniable chemistry. He was the perfect straight man to whatever crazy shit I was doing, and we started getting to that sweet spot onscreen where we could finish each other's sentences. When Don Rickles was asked about his partnership with Bob Newhart, Don said, "Here was this Catholic guy from the Midwest and I was this Jewish kid from Queens, it shouldn't have worked but it did, we were just so different, it was funny." Well, I was a Jewish kid from Manhattan and Drake was some kinda Christian from Orange County, so maybe it was the same secret sauce.

Drake and I sort of became this unstoppable force and before long we were literally in every scene together. It made no sense because, like I said, we couldn't have been more different. Drake liked the Beach Boys, I liked the Beastie Boys. Drake liked Mexican food, and for a thirteen-year-old weighing 220, Mexican was literally the only food I would turn down. But did Michael Jordan question Dennis Rodman for piercing his nipples and dying his hair blond? Nope, because he knew he'd always get the rebound. Not sure which one of us is Rodman in this scenario but you get what I'm saying.

On the court, we were magic.

One day, Dan Schneider, the creator of *The Amanda Show*, *All That*, *Kenan and Kel* (another spin-off of *All That*), and pretty much every other show you watched as a kid got a call from Nickelodeon. "We want another buddy comedy, something for the eight thirty time slot. Got any ideas?" Dan took this in, thought about it, and replied, "Nope."

Whelp, that was that.

From what Dan has told me, Drake and I definitely *did not* come to mind when the question was posed. And it's fine, I'm over it. Nevertheless, a few weeks later as Drake and I were filming our last scene of the season, a scene in which we were fighting over a giant shrimp, because of course, one of the writers walked up to Dan at the monitors and said, "Don't they want you to write a buddy comedy? There're your buddies." That writer's name is Steve Molaro, and in a long line of lucky breaks, this was another one. Thank you, Steve.

Six months later we were filming the pilot for *Drake & Josh*, my own TV show. I was fifteen, it felt like a second ago I was in that apartment with my mom going broke, wondering how I was going to save us, and now, well, it was just very different.

Over the next five years we shot sixty episodes and two movies. I was fifteen when it started, nineteen when it finished. It was high school for me—and my sentiments toward the show mimicked that of a high school experience. In the moment, there were times when I just wanted it to be over, but now I look back on the experience fondly, appreciating all that it gave me.

The concept was simple, two incredibly different guys are thrust into each other's lives as stepbrothers when their parents remarry, and they have to figure out how to live together. It was about family and people could relate, I think that's why almost fifteen years later, kids are still discovering the show through reruns, and adults look back on it fondly.

I know some of you reading this book might be interested in the doldrums of what happened on the set, the stories, the drama (which there wasn't much of), what it was like to have a hit show on television at sixteen. But for me, it didn't have much of an impact. I mean we were a hit show, sure, but kids' TV shows weren't the star-making factories they are today. It was kind of just a job. Don't get me wrong, a great job, one in which I was getting to perform my favorite kind of comedy, but when we wrapped, I'd go home to an apartment complex and watch hockey with my friend who lived in my building.

We all have an affinity for the dramatic, and why shouldn't we? Life for most is a monotonous slog toward the finish line with brief distractions along the way. The comedian Marc Maron once said, "If it's not cake or cumming, I'm really not interested." So who could blame us for looking at the people we watch, the athletes, the actors, etc., and believing or hoping that their existence is any different?

We romanticize process, we want to watch Kobe score the game-winning three-pointer, not the footwork drills he did every morning. We imagine a writer sitting down in front of a typewriter, half drunk on cheap wine and raw passion, firing away at the keys until the sun comes up. Instead of the realities of writing, which for most is a mind-numbing process of procrastination, missed deadlines, and never-ending edits that I wouldn't know anything about.

So what am I saying??

What I'm saying is that it would be reasonable to presume, like I did, that once someone books a TV show, one with their name in it, something fewer than a hundred people in history can lay claim to, that everything from that moment would be figured out. That once you were allowed past the gilded walls of success, some sort of immunity would be granted and the trappings, the mundanity of life would become null and void.

That wasn't true, not for me at least.

When I was nineteen and the show was over, it was time to prove myself again. There was no social media, so, it's not like you had this asset you'd acquired where you could take your followers with you once it was over. The red carpet didn't get rolled out, you weren't set for life. You were the star of a "kids'" show, a good show of course, but a kids' show nonetheless and it just didn't have the same cachet as something for grown-ups; in fact, in some cases it was a strike against you.

The people working around me at the time assumed that Drake and I would continue on as this unstoppable force, this comedic team, but there wasn't really a clear path for that once the show was over. Both of us, keenly aware of the challenge that lay ahead, thought better we split up, each man for himself. The world wanted to believe that we still shared a bedroom even if we weren't filming the TV show, but once that was over, so was our connection. It was like camp, eventually everyone has to go home.

Our names would become synonymous with each other forever. It's a long life but there's certainly a chance that *Drake & Josh* will be the most noteworthy thing either of us ever do. You can't choose what triggers the zeitgeist, what implants itself in the minds of the masses, and that's not necessarily a bad thing. Jim Carrey is one of our most talented performers alive and without question has done work that far surpasses his early comedic performances, but how good is *Ace Ventura*?! This is why Billy Joel won't play "Uptown Girl" anymore; you can't choose your hits, man!

This perhaps could explain why over a decade after the show ended, the world went insane when I got married and didn't invite Drake to my wedding. Now when I say insane I mean it in its most literal sense, in that people were "in a state of mind which prevents normal perception." People couldn't fathom that we'd only seen each other a handful of times since the show ended; they insisted that they had just seen us together, wackily trying to escape a tree house with no doors.

Similarly, when Drake got into legal trouble, people ran to get my opinion. They thought I must have a take on this person I had spent so much time with, when in reality, it had been years since we'd talked and even longer since we'd seen each other. Which is why alongside everyone else who doesn't know Drake, I was upset by the inexplicable events that unfolded in his life.

I'll probably get in trouble for this next sentence. But being a successful kid actor is kind of like doing porn. You can be super successful and make money doing it but when it's over, what do you do? OF COURSE there are examples of those who have transitioned to adulthood successfully but for every Shia LaBeouf or Zendaya, there are a thousand stories of burned-out former kid stars who inform the collective opinion. There's always going to be that stigma, that presumption that we know who you are because we saw you grow up.

I hate to talk about money but I just want to give you an accurate picture of where I was financially when the show ended. Drake and I started the show making $10k per episode and finished the show making $20k, so let's say the median per episode was $15k. Times that by sixty episodes and you've got $900k. Not bad. Except remove 20 percent for agent and manager fees and another 30 percent for Uncle Sam and you've got $450k. Still not bad. But spread that over five years, which is how long it took us to shoot all sixty episodes, and it breaks down to a little less than $100k a year. I'm not complaining, I'm just trying to give you an idea of where I was when the show ended. I needed to work and quickly because most of that money had gone to supporting my mom and me.

Oh, and kids' television doesn't pay residuals, which is super cute.

I knew I had my work cut out for me, I knew that in some instances it was worse to have been on television the past five years because producers had an image of who they thought you were and until someone was willing to take a chance on you, that image was impossible to break. I wasn't set for life, it wasn't like being the kid from *Modern Family* or *Stranger Things*, it was niche, a cable kids' show without a golden parachute. I didn't care, I couldn't care. No one's concerned with how well you played in college; if you don't make it to the pros, then you didn't make it.

I was ready, I had to be, I had already devoted literally half of my life to this, and my mom and my security depended on it. I had pulled off the impossible. I got us out of New York, I was on television, we weren't broke anymore. I took my life into my own hands and the results were miraculous.

Funny thing about taking your life into your own hands, though, is once you have it, there's no one to blame. It's now solely your responsibility to make something happen and if it all falls apart, well, that's on you. And that's exactly what happened, when I set my life on fire.

5

Fear and Loathing in Beverly Hills

The first time I did drugs was because of a girl.

The fiftieth time I did drugs, I was speeding down Cold-water Canyon, a thoroughfare that separates Beverly Hills from the San Fernando Valley, going a healthy clip above the speed limit. It was 8:00 a.m., and five hours prior, I had been ingesting copious amounts of dark-colored liquor and bright-colored prescription pills on what was quickly becoming just another weeknight. I had been living like this for a year now without much slowing down.

Drugs and alcohol were like a water truck in the middle of the desert for me, a respite from a life trudging along dehydrated, and I wasn't about to spite God for what was obviously a miracle. My entire life, my mind has been searching for relief, an antidote, some sort of brain bandage to quiet it. To lessen the pain of reality, of circumstance, of existence. I had food, of course, and that worked for a while; women were great but not always a sure thing;

success should have worked but it turned out to be not the powerful drug I thought it would be. It all worked to a point, but nothing, and I mean NOTHING worked as spectacularly as drugs and alcohol.

I'll never forget when I took my first drink. I'm not talking a few secret sips of table wine at a holiday dinner. I'm talking a proper guzzle of some firewater—stolen from a friend's parents' liquor cabinet—and the feeling it gave me the moment it hit my belly. It was like an invisible weight had been lifted, like parts of my lungs were unlocked and I could finally take a deep breath, a feeling as though for the first time in my life, everything was okay. It was revelatory.

Racing over the canyon, I figured the five hours of grace between me and my last drink was more than enough time to properly sober up and drive like a gentleman. Apparently I was wrong.

Apparently my driving was so erratic that the person behind me felt compelled to come up to my window and strongly suggest I get out of my car. Let me be more clear, when we finally stopped at a light, the guy behind me got out of his car and started punching my window, trying to literally rip me from my luxury sedan. Now, of course, being the level-headed, situation-defusing person I was at that time, I decided not to exit my vehicle and, instead, stay housed safely behind its steel walls.

This did not go over well with my new friend, who was now using a tool to breach my vehicular cocoon. I know!

I was just as surprised as you are. Here I was trying to

run a quick errand, and this derelict felt it necessary to completely overreact to what must have been a couple of missed turn signals at best! I tried to drive off, but it seemed the other motorists were in on it too because they started using their cars to box me in like it was '94 and I was in a white Bronco. I pushed down hard on the gas, drove over what I immediately realized was the front lawn of the Beverly Hills Hotel, and arrived safely on a side street bordering the hotel.

Now, most people in this scenario would have been happy to survive what was a scary and potentially violent situation, but I am not most people. I was at the height of my insanity, and my best thinking told me that the cogent thing to do at a time like this would be to alert law enforcement. Of course! Here I was, a model citizen, accosted on the mean streets of Beverly Hills. I couldn't leave this unreported!

What if another strung-out child star ran into a similar gang of pirates?!

As my car left the front lawn of the Beverly Hills Hotel, my fingers started dialing 911, and I began telling the operator exactly what had happened. Now, I was prepared to receive a hero's welcome from the operator along with some plans about where and when I would be receiving the keys to the city when I was promptly interrupted, "Sir, we've received seven calls about you in the past ten minutes. Pull your car over. We've got officers en route." Fuck.

There are moments in life when the universe takes out

a God-size needle of adrenaline and stabs you through the heart, à la John Travolta in *Pulp Fiction*, and this was one of those moments. I immediately hung up because this was all too real, all too quick, and it was time to make some snap decisions before I found myself with an incredibly unflattering mugshot on a collection of unflattering websites.

I looked around, realizing I was at the bottom of the foothills that separate Beverly Hills from the San Fernando Valley, and if I could somehow, some way, make it over the canyon and out of the Beverly Hills Police jurisdiction, there'd be a chance I could get away. And that's what happened, I drove a few blocks over and got away. I didn't even celebrate when I arrived safely at home, I just got in bed and went to sleep. I was exhausted, drugs are exhausting. The thing about roller coasters is you never know exactly when you're upside down, you just pray you make it back to the platform. I was upside down and had been for a while now.

A quick caveat, if you're looking for a drug memoir this ain't it. Go buy Anthony Kiedis's book *Scar Tissue* if you really want a beat-by-beat thrill ride through the garden of mind-altering substances. For me, the sordid details are less important than how the drugs *actually* worked for me, why I did them, and how I eventually stopped doing them. Plus, my mom's still alive and will probably purchase this book, at a discount obviously, friends and family.

So I've already told you why I liked doing drugs, but

why did I *start* doing drugs in the first place? Because I lost 100 pounds obviously.

You don't get to 297 pounds at sixteen because you're perfectly content. I can tell you that much. You get there because you hate yourself, or God, or your parents, or something else living deep within your secret place. And if you manage to do the unthinkable and actually lose 100 pounds—127, to be exact—you might find yourself with a new body and the exact same self-hating mind.

The blood-brain barrier is a miracle of nature's engineering. It's a literal anatomical wall created by the body to keep things away from the super computer that is your brain. This is why it's incredibly hard to treat brain cancer with chemotherapy, because the body is hell-bent on keeping things out, even if they're good for it.

I think the blood-brain barrier is a perfect metaphor for this time in my life. Here I was at eighteen. I had lost all this weight (how, you'll find out soon, I promise) and for the first time in my life I was in control of my eating. I had done it. I had moved to California, gotten a job, made some money, and now I'd lost the weight that I felt was holding me back. Things were looking good for me . . . but my mind hadn't caught up yet. It was holding on tight to the idea that I was still powerless, that the world was unfair, that I had to reach for something to comfort myself. My brain hadn't accepted my new reality, it still thought we were fighting.

So there was that, 100 pounds lighter, but with a broken

brain in a new body, I was the Scarecrow from *The Wizard of Oz*. And then there was this other part, something far more common and definable.

I was young and supremely stupid.

As I was coming up on my eighteenth birthday, I had gone from 297 pounds to just below 200. I was getting really close to my goal weight and it seemed I'd gotten in just at the buzzer. I was going to be able to spend the best years of my life as a thin person. Thank you, God.

I was eighteen, I was excited to experience all the things I didn't know how to try as an overweight kid—such as going to a party, swimming without a shirt on, or kissing a girl. It was time to cash in on some life stock and truly get stupid. So when I met a sweet-faced nineteen-year-old girl, let's call her Jessica, even though we both know that's not her name, I was helpless. She liked me and I liked her, or at the very least, I liked being liked and I was prepared to do anything to make sure that didn't change.

That's how I found myself sitting in the poorly furnished living room of some guy named Rick, watching as Jessica removed some powder-like substance from a little Baggie as her gaggle of mean girlfriends sat waiting their turn. "Oh my God this is so good, Mike always has the best stuff," she said. Until that point I'd never seen drugs in person, not really. I mean this was cocaine, a proper drug, the kind they warn you about when a police officer comes to your elementary school.

I sat there watching as she gave me a master class in ingesting intoxicants. She wiped her face, looked up, and said, "You want some?" Like it was M&M's.

"Do I want some?" Mean girls one and two looked at me like I was ten years old, frozen at the end of a diving board. Jessica, on the other hand, stared at me lovingly like a lifeguard, assuring me she'd jump in if I swallowed too much water. I shifted uncomfortably. "Oh um, no thanks, I'll pass on the schedule one narcotics." Come on, Peck! You've been waiting for this moment your entire life and you answered like an undercover cop with Tourette's?! Okay, I didn't say that, but I'm sure that's what it sounded like. I had never even seen drugs before, let alone declined them.

All you need to know is, I said no. A hard no, a no for the ages, the kind of no you give a telemarketer, sorry, I have no interest in extending my car's warranty. She shrugged and dove in for more. Luckily, drug users, in my experience, tend to be unbothered when they don't have to share.

Your body craves what it needs, it's why Gatorade tastes so good when you're dehydrated, shout out Gatorade. With its perfect blend of H_2O, sugar, and electrolytes, your body sops the stuff up like free drinks at the club. I think that's the reaction I had that night, I remember watching Jessica's eyes after her first hit and noticing the relief she felt after taking it. There was no way I could've known what she was feeling, I'd never done it before, but relief?

My brain could recognize relief. That night has become important, because it's the last time I had a choice in the matter. I said no. I almost escaped. I almost made it out alive except my mind wrote a rain check that night. Under the right circumstance, eventually, I knew I'd say yes.

The speed at which the right circumstance presents itself tends to be quick when you're ready to do bad things, because a few nights later, when it was just her and me, no friends, no one around, just two star-crossed lovers and a felony's worth of drugs between us, I said yes. A resounding yes. I couldn't have known what I was signing myself up for, I didn't know my life would never be the same. I just . . . I just hoped she was watching.

Let's back up for a second.

I grew up filming *Drake & Josh* in a transient apartment complex in Los Angeles. The kind of place you live in if you're giving showbiz a try, or drug dealing, or both. The kind of place you go after your divorce wipes you out and you're left with that leather couch she never liked. The majority of people who live in this apartment complex sign a six-month lease, try to book a TV show, or literally do anything to avoid moving back to their hometown. This was where I spent my formative years, fourteen through longer than I'd like to admit, in an oasis of child actors, divorcées, and drug dealers. It wasn't that it was cheap; it just attracted a clientele that needed a short lease and those kinds of people tend to be short leased in all areas of their life. To be honest, my mom and I were just stoked on the amenities.

I was in the hot tub of that apartment complex one fateful night, my new body nestled safely under the bubbles, when a group of what looked look like today would be TikTok stars entered the pool area. Normally, I would've wrapped myself up in a towel and waddled back to my apartment but this night, this night was different. I was eighteen, fresh-faced, and ready to act my age. I was on television, people did invite me places. It's not that I didn't have opportunities to go out, it's just, I never did. *One day*, I thought as I alphabetized my DVDs.

I struck up a conversation with those kids and, within a week, I was following them to every club and house party in Hollywood. I had arrived, I was doing it, young people shit, how thrilling. Were these my friends? Not sure. It gives me cringe chills to think about all of those parties now but back then I mean, what can I say? I had been working since I was ten, always driven by fear and panic, eye on the prize, *don't do anything to jeopardize your career* constantly running through my brain. I was due some bad behavior, right? I was dying to be reckless, to be frivolous, these kids had connections and I had a car and money, it was a match made in heaven.

Jessica was a part of my new crew and that's how we wound up getting high together a few weeks later.

Back to the bathroom.

She laid some cocaine in front of me, its glimmering goodness sparkling bright like an oasis on a CD case. I took a beat, waiting for an act of God to disrupt us, an earthquake, SOMETHING to dissuade me, but it never came. Thanks for the green light, God!

I was excited to do it, wondering how cool and mature I must've looked. To be honest, the drug was of no interest to me, it was the act of doing it that seemed to me to be the most exciting part, and what it meant to be entering the ranks of people such as Kurt Cobain, such as Hunter S. Thompson, such as Basquiat. I wasn't a fat loser anymore, I was a misunderstood drug user, and that sounded *infinitely* sexier to me. Cool people did drugs, Jessica did drugs, and I wanted to do them too.

I felt it whoosh through my nostrils and set up shop near my frontal cortex. I waited for the effects to hit me, I tried to look comfortable, like I'd been there before. Our eyes met, I waited for her to say something like "Mission accomplished" or "Welcome" or "You were never fat to me" but it never came, she just anxiously dove in for more. I waited for the effects to hit, for that wave of euphoria to wash over me, for God's hand to start caressing my cheek. I actually didn't know what to expect but I'd been drunk before, was it going to be like that?

I waited and waited and waited and then waited some more, but nothing . . .

I felt . . . nothing.

I had thought maybe the effects would come on mildly, like my vision would blur, and as it peaked my heart would stop and I'd die, but LITERALLY NOTHING. Not a hallucination, not a rapid heartbeat, not even a giggle fit, I mean what good are drugs if not for a giggle fit? It didn't matter, I'd done it and she saw me do it, that's all I was concerned with.

I stood there, looking at Jessica, taking in this moment, completely undeterred by the fact that I was stone sober when all of a sudden I heard BANG BANG BANG on the door. Uh-oh. DEA? FBI? Nope, just Rick. "We're leaving!" he screamed. Jessica looked at me and asked, "Want to go to a party?" OF COURSE I want to go to a party, that's what people do when they've just done drugs and far be it from me to break precedent. This was all going so well. At that moment, I wasn't different, I was *typical*. God it felt good to be typical.

We loaded into a car, half past the time of night when young people do bad things, and headed to some rooftop in Hollywood. At this point I was still waiting to feel something, ANYTHING. As we arrived, I couldn't help but think, *Maybe drugs don't work on me, ya know, the way redheads are super healers?*

We arrived and I don't know if it's because I'd just learned I was a drug ginger, but I really enjoyed myself, it was the best party I'd ever been to. The drinks were good, the music was good, and I was good. I spent the night mingling, telling jokes, chopping it up with random strangers, making Jessica laugh, this is what I'd signed up for, baby! I was the goddamn TikTok star that night!

As I climbed into bed, replaying the events of the evening, I lay there in the afterglow, thinking about how well it had gone and how far I'd come. This is what I'd always wanted, I was living it. I was overcome by this feeling of peace, of contentment, as though I had conquered a summit I had been training for my entire life and was taking in the view. It was beautiful.

And then I realized something. It was the drugs.

A warning to potential drug abusers near and far, past and present, current and in training. If when you ingest narcotics, you feel more like yourself than when you are sober, when the feeling is so comfortable that you can't think of why you'd ever want to feel another way, you, my friend, are *screwed*. Drugs lifted the pain of existence so well that I mistook being high for being alive.

This goes back to the first conceit of this book, that we are all an amalgamation of trauma. If you've spent your entire life carrying an invisible backpack full of metaphorical stones around, stones full of past experience, painful memory, and regret, then you shouldn't be surprised when your knees start to buckle under the undue weight of such impedimenta. And if you discovered by chance a magical potion that instantly made the weight of that knapsack just a little lighter, the shoulder straps just a little looser, why would you ever look anywhere else? You don't even have to examine the rocks! You might not have known the backpack was even on in the first place, all you KNOW is suddenly your legs don't hurt anymore. In fact, they feel great.

The events of that evening didn't make sense, they didn't track. I didn't LIKE parties, especially back then. I was always left reeling from some interaction gone wrong, some awkward moment that would send me into a tailspin about what an immense loser I was. Have you ever walked away from a conversation and regretted what you said? That was me, in all conversations all the time, and a party is a surplus of conversation! So who was this guy? This impostor? This TikTok star? Who was I?

This was high Josh, and high Josh is great at parties.

I'd finally found a kind of medicine that night. It was a medicine I'd been searching for my entire life, a cure that allowed me to be me. Not the me that was worried about what you thought, it was the me I had always wanted to project. Someone so effortlessly cool and secure that I couldn't be bothered by my past, I have no past! Present, here and now, I don't make apologies because there's nothing to apologize for, life is good and so am I.

"The lie we tell ourselves is, as I am, I am not enough." Well, that night, I was enough.

The change was subtle, it took a few nights like this one before I noticed a change. I didn't sleep, my jaw hurt, but I felt great. I had expected to feel utterly out of control, unhinged, unsafe, but instead I felt the opposite. I'd never felt so in control. Drugs made reality more palatable. I didn't know I had awoken a beast, this phenomenon of craving, this virus that wouldn't be happy until its host was dead.

I just thought I was finally getting some relief.

Someone once asked me what it felt like to be addicted to drugs and this is how I described it: "Imagine you've spent your entire life trying to listen to a radio station, but every time you tuned in, there was static. You were certain you were on the right frequency, but the signal was never very strong. And then one day, you accidentally bump the knob and suddenly all the auditory goodness you've been waiting to hear your entire life fills your ears, in surround sound. You had been on the wrong wavelength but not anymore. That's what drugs felt like for me, I wasn't tuning out, I was tuning in."

A thought came to me while lying in bed that night that ignited the most corrosive period of my life. *If this is possible, why would I ever want to feel another way?* And that's how I spent the next four years, chasing that feeling and ruining everything in the process.

6

What Does That Say About God?

I didn't see a picture of my dad until I was twenty-four.

January 2013. I was driving home. I couldn't help but notice heavy raindrops exploding on my windshield. I should have known something was up, it never rains in LA.

Mom called.

Mom: Hey.
Me: Hi, what's going on?
Mom: So I have some bad news, honey.
Me: Uh-oh. Okay.
Mom: I'm sorry to tell you this, but your dad passed away.

I guess she had Googled his name and an obituary came up. 'Bye, Dad.

Earlier that day, my mom and I had met up for lunch and the conversation of my father came up, as it tended to every now and then. I think it was between appetizers and entrées that I mentioned, not for the first time, that perhaps I would go try to find him. I knew the city where he lived through some random Googling, his last two addresses, that was about it but it was a start. I had spent most of my life completely against the idea of meeting him but something, something was softening my resolve.

I was twenty-six, and while I surely had more living to do, there was a part of me that thought, *If not now, when?* Actually, I think Hillel the Elder said that first, but if your Ancient Jewish Scholar game isn't on point, I'll gladly take credit. I think I was less scared because I had actually grown up, I mean kind of, at the very least I had achieved the height and weight of a fully grown man. So I knew that no matter what happened, my life didn't have to be radically altered by meeting him, not if I didn't want it to be. I think as a kid, I was too afraid of what might come of it. What if he wanted me to quit acting? What if he wanted me to come live with him? What if Mom's feelings were hurt? I just didn't want to invite more uncertainty into what was already a life chock full of it.

As I mentioned, I didn't see a picture of my father till I was twenty-four. TWENTY-FOUR. It's one thing not to meet your parent but it's another not to even know what they look like, it's maddening. I think we naturally look to our parents as evolutionary guides, their faces, their personalities all clues as to where we came from and where we're going, but growing up without a dad was like having half of that lesson missing.

Mom, please don't read this next paragraph.

Growing up I desperately wanted to be different from my mother. Perhaps this isn't a new idea, you'd be hard pressed to find any teen who doesn't seriously rebel against their genetic inheritance. My mom was overweight, I was overweight—she was the artistic, nonconforming black sheep of almost any situation and I was the unathletic, not masculine enough, weirdo actor kid who desperately wanted to fit in, blend in. I'd take whatever version of "in" was available. And because I only had her as a reference, my future of being just like her felt inescapable. I'd grow up to appreciate all those qualities about her later, but as a kid they were less attractive.

Most of my childhood was spent navigating lose-lose situations when it came to my dad. I'd either feel left out of some father/son event that I couldn't attend or worse, I *could* attend but as the third wheel to whichever friend's dad let me tag along. Of course there were the well-intentioned yet completely boundary-free dads who would look at me and make grand declarations such as "Josh, think of me as your father!" It seemed the only reason they said that though was so they could yell at me like they did their own kids, it was never to include me in allowance day.

Because I knew so little about my father, I took artistic liberties when it came to describing him, as a weird consolation prize. It's like fantasizing about what you'd do with lottery money. When people would ask me where he's from I'd say "Morocco" or "Spain" or "Israel," somewhere exotic. I basically just picked places that would explain my dark curly hair and olive skin. The guy definitely wasn't from Norway, I knew that much. When people would ask if I had siblings I'd say, "Yup, three, two sisters and a brother." Which was true, I DO have three half siblings, I've just never met them and if they're reading this, allow me to say "Nice to meet you and sorry I exist"?

Early on, the desire to meet my dad was nonexistent. It wasn't anger, it was apathy; I just didn't miss what I never had. I was mad at God, but I wasn't mad at my dad. Every missed Father's Day or Boy Scout meeting, Little League practice or talent show, I didn't wish my dad was there, I just cursed the universe for putting me in this predicament. I was mad at God for everything else seemingly out of my control, being fat, broke, scared, so not having a father just seemed like another way of the universe saying, "Of course you don't have one, that would be far too normal for you, loser."

I also knew on some level that perhaps I was being spared. I've known plenty of men in my life who've said, "You never met your dad? Fuck, I wish I never met MY dad." I grew up in New York City, mind you, surrounded by city kids like me from lower-middle-class backgrounds, so I wasn't the only kid navigating weird father waters. We weren't the majority by any means but I knew more than a few kids who either didn't know their dad, or did know them but they were in and out of their lives, leaving wreckage every time they popped their heads in. Dads, am I right?

Evolutionary scientists talk about how babies are more likely to be born looking like their father and also possess that sweet baby smell so that the father is less likely to leave. Oh, I'm sorry, DARWIN, but are you kidding me? The relationship between a kid and their father is so tenuous that if they dare resemble their mother or don't possess the sweet smell of *eau du bébé*, they might have to risk living without a father forever? This seems uniquely fucked up.

As I got older and started focusing on my career, I was happy to have only one parent, because as I've said before, my mom was uniquely suited for this thrill ride that is show business. I knew that we were headed on a misadventure and there was a high likelihood that another parental figure involved in the decision-making process might have brought some understandable amounts of caution to this whole thing. "Hold on, you're going to quit school to do what? Get your head out of the clouds, kid."

Who knows? Maybe he would've been the best and my childhood would have been a never-ending game of catch with what I assume is a very Jewish-looking Richard Gere. You just don't know. What I do know is that I was going full speed toward this career of mine, and I didn't have time for any uninvited pragmatism.

At a certain age I just turned off whatever pain I felt about the whole dad thing, it was old. I was tired of being the dadless kid. I rationalized all the reasons I was better off. I had a career, I had one parent who loved me, perhaps too much! Dads only care about how you smell, right? Of course, "turning off the pain" doesn't actually deal with it, it just starts to burn like the embers of a poorly extinguished campfire. It's fine, it probably won't set your tent on fire ... or it might burn down the whole forest.

There's a line in *Fight Club* where Brad Pitt says, "Our fathers were our models for God. If our fathers bailed, what does that tell you about God?" It's a great line, one rife with all the delicious drama of a great movie, but it does touch on something worth exploring. What kind of imprinting happens when the first person who was supposed to love you, leaves?

How did this manifest? you might ask. I'll put you in touch with some ex-girlfriends (of whom there are not many). I think they can all attest that when the going got tough, Josh got going. That's right, everyone! I was quickly following in the footsteps of my fleeing father, destined to perpetuate his bad behavior at the first sign of trouble. Things would be going great, because what's better than regular sex with a new person, and then there would be the whisper of an issue, the hint of trouble, and I would just bail. Better I leave you before you leave me, in fact, let me show you how good I am at leaving and how little I needed you at all. Usually this would leave the girl contemplating what went wrong. "He said he wanted Chinese, I said I was in the mood for Thai, and then he just left?" I just wasn't capable of enduring the natural conflicts that arise when you're in a relationship. They weren't necessary growing pains for me, they were harbingers of more bad to come.

Similarly, my relationships with men were *no bueno*. I don't know how long it took me to realize that I was putting almost every man in my life in a surrogate father position. Unbeknownst to them and myself, I was psychically elevating any and every man in my life, literally even Frankie, the doorman of our apartment building, to the position of father figure and attaching all the expectations that came with it. When Frankie would eventually disappoint me, as of course he did, he didn't agree to this secret agreement I drew up between my ears, I would become resentful and retaliate. *I knew it, you're just like the rest,* I thought. *You're probably opening doors for other eight-year-olds all over town!*

The truth is, I was angry. I was an angry young man and there are few archetypes more literary than the angry young man. Hamlet was angry, so was Holden Caulfield, I'd be nervous if I met a young person who wasn't. This anger was burning dirty, though. As my friend Brian Koppelman said, it kept my car going but it was ruining my engine. I could feel even in my late teens that there was something amiss here, that I seemed to be getting into these recurring situations first with men, and then in my twenties with women, that all had the same outcome. I ran away resentful and they were left not knowing what happened.

This was the impetus for the first major change in my

life. I'll talk about exactly how I came to this and how I began to work on it in the next chapter, but for the sake of staying on subject, let's skip ahead to what happened after that big change.

I had successfully made it into my midtwenties without ever having met my dad. I was well into my career, even if it was far from skyrocketing, and while I wasn't always happy, I knew on a fundamental level that I was decent, and that there was still time for my life to turn out exactly as I'd hoped.

You've probably forgotten by now, but as I mentioned, my father was sixty-two when he got my mom pregnant. I mean there was no discounting this senior, he was getting Medicare AND chicks pregnant. But I digress. So by the time I was twenty-five, he was eighty-seven. It's really hard to be a young eighty-seven, we ain't talking about Ruth Bader Ginsburg here, we're talking about an old Jew who retired to Florida decades earlier.

So when the idea of meeting my dad would cross my mind, I would think, *Well, I know what he gets, a good kid who doesn't really need anything from him.* I had lost a hundred pounds, had some money in my pocket—I had become a man, a flawed man, a man who still had a shitload of work to do on himself, but a man nonetheless and it wasn't easy. So that's what he got, a good kid who needed nothing from him except maybe an apology and an explanation.

But what did I get? The sands of time had made it so that

I would inherit this geriatric father, an INVALID. We were never going to play catch, we'd missed it. At best maybe we'd have some good conversation but if I was going to go for it, I wanted the FDE, the FULL DAD EXPERIENCE, can't I get a little reciprocity here? Okay, I'm dramatizing it slightly, I'm not sure I thought that deeply about it, but I think the truth is, despite my curiosity, I didn't want him to enjoy the spoils—I didn't want him to be proud of a kid he had nothing to do with. And I don't know how to feel about that.

It's frustrating at times to think that my dad not only brought me into this world, but also LEFT this world completely on his own terms. I really had no say in the matter. I know I've already said this once, but I gotta give it to the guy, when he set his mind to something, he really saw it through. When he said he didn't want anything to do with me, he meant it. It was sort of his last stand, I don't know if I ever would have sought him out, if I ever would have met him, but ya know what? It was nice having the option, it was powerful, like holding this emotional grenade I could unleash on his life at any moment.

It was after my father's passing that a deep curiosity was ignited in me. I just needed to know more about him.

One day I was tooling around Facebook, using it for its intended purpose, to spy on people's lives, not to spread disinformation, the way it is today, and I decided to plug my sister's name into the search box. As I said, I knew I had half siblings who were grown, much older than I was, because my mom and dad were friends before they were (shiver) lovers. He TALKED about his family with her, right until his well-timed pretend separation. I loved the idea that I had siblings out there, I dreamed of the day I might meet them, thinking, *I hope it's not too late for bunk beds.*

In the past, I had always sought my father out, but because of his age, he didn't have much of an online footprint. It wasn't until it occurred to me to potentially try my sibling's name that things really opened up. I typed her name into the search bar and in an instant a few pictures popped up, all with the same name. I did some scrolling and there she was, approximate age looked right, she lived in the same state as my dad, and oh right, we looked alike. Her page was private, though, we had no friends in common except for a dad, so that was that. Well, not really.

I showed my best friend, Len, the profile a few days later, lamenting like a detective who hit a dead end, when his older brother Garri came strolling in and noticed something on the screen, like a missed clue in a crime scene. "Says she attended a workshop I've been to." In the interest of protecting her privacy, I won't say which workshop, but just imagine it was a Tony Robbins type of weekend retreat. Okay, Sis, we love a queen who betters herself! "I'll try to friend her, see what happens."

A few days later I received the text. "We're in, bro, I'm friends with your sister, get over here." I raced over to Len and Garri's house and what I found next was like my own personal Rosetta Stone. Suddenly I was flooded with imagery of my father. Until this point, the only picture I'd ever seen was of him at a wedding that a friend of a friend gave me the year before. It was blurry and the picture was of the entire wedding, a gigantic group photo of all the attendants, so yeah not exactly HD. Cut to me perusing my sister's Facebook page and gorging myself on an entire treasure trove of snapshots.

There were pictures of my dad as a young man, pictures of him at bar mitzvahs and birthday parties, playing catch with his kids, and at holiday dinners. There were pictures of him and my siblings with captions that read, "We love you, Dad, miss you every day." There were tributes on her Facebook wall about what a good man he was and what an impact he had on their lives. From what I could tell, this man was loved and revered by his children, he was all the things I wish he could've been for me, for them.

It was then that I began to get the closure I didn't know I needed, to truly say good-bye to my dad. I can't believe I had to mourn a man I never knew and without all the requisite deli trays that accompany a good Jewish funeral.

Looking at my sister's Facebook page showed me this wasn't some serial adulterer with a bunch of bastard kids around (that I know of), this was a flawed man who made a mistake. A scared guy who, when given the choice, decided to do what he thought was right for his family. It might not have been the Ultimate right, but I can't be the arbiter of that. People ask me if I have any desire to meet my siblings. I assume they don't know I exist otherwise they would've found me, I mean . . . I'm not exactly hiding. But my answer is always no, I just have no desire to blow up whatever illusion they have of their dad. Because my existence doesn't disqualify who he was to them, and while I might have experienced a different side of the same man, I'm not sure what's to be gained by rocking their world.

All these feelings came back a decade later when my son Max was born. I was terrified to have a boy. My wife and I decided to go old school and not find out the sex of the baby till he was born, so I had nine months to think about it. Some might say if God intended for us to know the sex of the baby beforehand, he'd have put a window in the mom's belly—either way I highly suggest waiting to find out, there are just so few surprises in life. Anyway, while I hoped and prayed I'd have a girl, figuring I'd done so much musical theater in my life it was practically a lock, I knew on some deep-seated level I would have a boy.

Why? Because this was my cosmic comeuppance. I had to correct the negative cycle, this feedback loop created by generations of dysfunction before me. I was terrified to have a son because I didn't think I knew how to raise a boy, I had no model for it. Still to this day, I cringe near a basketball court at the mere thought of someone casually passing me the ball and saying, "Put it up."

But then I had to remember what a friend of mine had told me, "Your job as a father is to tell your kid, I know it's scary and you might get hurt, but ya gotta do it anyway and I'll be with you the whole way." Pretty sure he meant that specifically for teaching a kid how to ride a bike, but still, I took it to heart. If facing your fears, doing things scared, and walking through discomfort was a major tenet of fatherhood, then I knew how to do that. I couldn't insulate him from pain but I could be there to support him while he endured it.

I had to be for him what I wished my dad was for me, because sometimes the only way to correct trauma is by not passing it to the next victim. We don't always get the amends we deserve, but maybe we give it to ourselves when we put an end to the behavior. By being good to my kid, I was honoring eight-year-old Josh, who felt so left out and alone.

There were moments when my son was just a few weeks old, when the lack of sleep makes you feel like you have a low-grade hangover all day, that I would just stare at him as he slept, drank his bottle, cried, sneezed, ya know—baby shit. I knew I was far from doing it perfectly, but I was there, I was present for all of it except for the moments when my saint of a mother-in-law would take him for the night. I loved it all, the wake-ups, the diapers, the doctors' visits, and the thought crossed my mind more than once that my dad missed all of this.

And I felt bad for him.

7

Daddy Gandhi

I'm a twenty-year-old drug addict standing in Times Square with Ben Kingsley.

Ben Kingsley is Gandhi. LITERALLY a knight. *Sir Ben Kingsley.* He is my hero. I know for most people it's Tom Brady or Michelle Obama but I'm an acting nerd, remember?

I fell in love with Sir Ben Kingsley when I was nine years old, watching the movie *Searching for Bobby Fischer* on repeat waiting for my mom to get home. As I got older, I watched him in *Sexy Beast, Schindler's List,* and anything else I could get my hands on, thinking, *Oh, THIS is great acting.* He's my favorite kind of actor, honoring the truth of the character without winking at the audience to win their favor. It's really hard to catch him acting, it's effortless.

The Wackness was a film directed by Jonathan Levine about an eighteen-year-old, hip-hop-loving, New York drug dealer played by me, who trades marijuana for therapy from a drugged-out, brilliant psychologist played by Kingsley. I was perfect for the role. I auditioned, praying I'd get the part but assuming there was no way because no one gets their first major acting role as an adult, opposite their favorite actor. Plus at the time I was routinely beaten out for roles by Michael Cera or Miles Teller, so it just seemed highly unlikely. Also, shout out Michael Cera and Miles Teller for being more talented than I was, good for you guys.

When I got the call that I had booked the movie, my manager got on the phone and asked, "Are you sitting down?" People only ask that when they have really good news or really bad news, and at that time it could have gone either way. But I knew I was the right guy. I had the advantage of actually being a hip-hop-loving, drug-addicted kid from New York, I knew how to do it.

Cut to two months later, Sir Ben and I are standing in Times Square at three in the morning, filming our last scene of the movie together. Filming until this point had gone incredibly well, considering I had spent the preceding three years doing my best Charlie Sheen impression. I had been unabashedly sowing the fuck out of my wild oats, fueled by a list of substances banned in most countries, but somehow, for the two months of filming, I kept it together. I had employed some internal governor that kept me from ruining this huge opportunity, and thank God, if I had blown this, I never would have forgiven myself. Every day I would show up to work for a master class with one of the best actors alive, my hero, acting in scenes together and being treated as an equal, not bad for a kid from Hell's Kitchen.

There was something I really wanted to ask Sir Ben when we started filming, something I needed to ask desperately but I just couldn't summon the courage. I was afraid of looking dumb. But with only a few minutes remaining on our last scene together, on the last day of shooting, I decided to throw a Hail Mary and go for it. I mean, when was I ever going to get this opportunity again?

"Got any advice?"

Remember not wanting to look dumb? Yeah, me too. In hindsight, I was probably still in my Josh-collecting-surrogate-father-figures stage. I was desperate, I wanted to know what the hell to do with my life. Was I going to be okay? Was anything going to be okay? Sure, things for the moment were great professionally but I also had a drug habit that was doing push-ups waiting to get me back, and I had literally been running on instinct for the past decade. If I'm honest, what I was really looking for was a reassuring male figure to tell me that I was doing okay, that everything was going to be okay, and how often do you have access to your hero?

He gave me a look like "You're really going to make me answer this?" I stared blankly, immediately regretting this and every other decision I had ever made in my life. He paused and then said, "Find your Apostles."

"Find your Apostles?"

I'm sorry, I'm Jewish, aren't "Apostles" more of a New Testament deep track? Apostles? What did that even mean? I was stunned into silence, not sure whether to just nod and walk away or ask my follow-up question of "Wha?" Thankfully, he kept going.

"Find the people who support you to be what you want to be, who push you to be your very best, and if you find yourself in a room with someone who doesn't make you feel that way, leave immediately."

It was good advice, the best kind of advice in fact because it's true no matter what. You can change the angle on it, you can put it through any lens, but it never becomes less true, less good.

Unfortunately, it took me ten years to understand what he meant. It was like handing a toddler the keys to a Bentley, they can't even open the door. What I was looking for was some hack of how to be the best actor in the world because I was pretty sure all of my problems would be solved as a result. I wasn't putting the cart before the horse, I was trying to inject the horse with steroids!

Didn't he understand that I was trying to find validation through the material world? That all I needed was success so I could make an example of anyone who ever doubted me while also securing so much financial freedom that I'd never *never* have to feel scared again? Didn't he get that?! I didn't need age-old wisdom, I needed results!

They say the teacher reveals himself when the student is ready. Well, I was still in the school staircase smoking cigs apparently. I told Sir Ben, "Thanks for the fortune cookie, but I'm searching for the secret to acting here, not a shaman in a sweat lodge." I probably didn't say that, I'm pretty sure I just thanked him and kept it moving, destined to go deeper into my self-centered quest for contentment.

While I was writing this book I researched the earliest use of the term "Apostles" and here's what I got. In the Bible, Jesus got a crew together of his twelve most loyal disciples, less Judas, who turned out to be a real dud (there's one in every group), to go around and spread the gospel. I mean, he might have been the Father, the Son, and the Holy Spirit, but at the time he was an up-and-coming new artist who needed some BUZZ. He couldn't be everywhere at once (or could he?). The Apostles were Jesus's grassroots marketing team, handing out flyers, posting signs, and getting the word out in a major way from Damascus to Bethlehem. They were his *Ride or Die* and *Ride Again* homies because of the Resurrection, which is an incredible name for a rap album.

The Greek translation of "Apostle," in its most literal sense, is an emissary or "one who is sent off," which is why the word "messenger" is a common alternative translation. We all love a messenger, especially if they're carrying an Edible Arrangement. But if that messenger is delivering an emotional truth, one we've been blind to, well that's slightly less exciting and surely less edible.

I'll tell you who the most recent Apostle was in your life, all you have to do is tell me the last person who pissed you off because you knew they were right. In my experience, the message from an Apostle is almost always met with opposition. If you were capable of hearing it, wouldn't you have come to it on your own? My reaction to almost every Apostle in my life has always been,

Screw them.

I'm the worst.

They might be right but it's too late anyway.

Okay, I'll try it.

And if those same sentiments go off in your head, ding ding ding, you, my friend, might have just found someone worth listening to.

I think Sir Ben in his wise, some might call it Gandhiesque, way knew that giving me people advice would serve me better than whatever generic life or career advice I thought I was looking for. Careers are fleeting, full of ups and downs, we know this, but the people you surround yourself with will be the consistent threads in your life. The network of people who offer you support will be the ones you not only lean on but also rejoice with forever, so it would behoove you to pick wisely. I THINK that's what he was trying to say.

Going forward in the book, I'm going to call out Apostles in my life, people who along the road to wherever I was headed offered me the kind of guidance I didn't know I needed, even when it hurt my feelings.

Before I go, I'll give you one more example.

My mom hates to fly. It's an issue. We've driven

cross-country six times and traversed back and forth via train more than that. If you ever want to have dinner at a place where the patrons are either senior citizens, Amish, or criminals, just head to your closest Amtrak dining car and head east. I hated these trips, mostly because they led to long, drawn-out conversations where we would discuss everything and anything that crossed our minds. I mean, what else were we going to do? I didn't mind the spending time with my mom part, what I minded was knowing that normal people flew places and that was just too regular for the Pecks.

I don't know what my mom saw in my teenage self when she said this somewhere between Albuquerque and Amarillo on Interstate 40, but in hindsight, it was truly Apostolic.

Mom: You're angry. **Me:** What?
Mom: You're angry. **Me:** I'm not angry.

I was angry, she was right, which made me more angry. I don't know what she saw that triggered her to say this. Maybe it was that I was seventeen and three hundred pounds. Maybe it was because I spent my summers driving cross-country with my mom instead of going to parties and being a teenager, maybe it was because I took it out on her. I don't know.

What I do know is that I had been angry for a really long time, I felt entitled to it because of the rough hand life dealt me. My anger was a warm blanket that kept the world at bay, and over time it had become almost imperceptible. The dirty little secret is that it's not about the outbursts, the bar fights, the fits of rage. Anger is about the quiet, seething judgment of everyone and everything. You become the self-appointed arbiter of all that is right and wrong in the world and if people would only act the way you thought they should, life would be infinitely better.

Fear is passive, it's reactionary. Anger is active, it's an offensive strike, it's the original hot take. My entire life, I so badly wanted to protect that powerless kid, the one who felt pushed around by the world and everyone in it. If the world was unfair, then I could be unfair right back, I'd show anyone who tried to disrespect me, belittle me, anyone who tried to treat me like the kid that I was instead of the man of my house, which I ALSO was, to regret ever looking at me the wrong way. When you're angry, everything is personal and nothing is random. You take on the injustice of the world, and if there's no injustice, you create it. It felt good to be on the offensive, powerful.

That anger kept me safe, protecting me from a world I was too sensitive for, it was an anchor in a sea of turmoil, a suit of armor that kept the world at bay. But if physics is right and every action has an equal and opposite reaction, it's no surprise that I found myself, in that moment, completely alone. I mean, my mom was there but she doesn't count. I had done such a good job of protecting myself that I had successfully insulated myself from everything the world had to offer, good and bad. You can walk around the forest in fear of a poisonous mushroom, but eventually if you don't eat something you'll starve.

I was clearly unhappy and the outward manifestation of that was how I looked. My mom could see that, because she's an Apostle and that's what Apostles do, they plant little truth trees in your brain and eventually a goddamn forest sprouts up and it's so fucking majestic that you can't ignore it anymore.

The last thing she said was this: "Josh, you gotta let go of this anger to move on with your life. I love you and always will because you're my son, but you will soon push people away if you don't confront this side of you."

When the student is ready, the teacher will reveal themselves. Damn it. She had gotten through, she'd wounded, but how? And why? Why now?

Why at this moment was I finally able to hear it?

Because the person I was angriest with was me. I was tired of looking like this, of feeling like this, of watching life pass me by. I knew I needed to make a change, I knew I had to lose the weight or die trying. Normal people don't do a quick math equation to see how much weight a chair can hold, it shouldn't require algebra to have a seat at dinner.

"Pain is knowledge rushing into your brain with great speed." My mom, my first Apostle.

8

Some Not Nice Things About Myself

I'm going to say some not nice things about myself here, some things that I was feeling at a time in my life when I was in a tremendous amount of pain. I want to reiterate that this is how I felt, it's not a commentary on anyone but me. I hope when you read this that it doesn't take away from body positivity or from anyone who feels utterly content in their own skin. My hat is off to you. I hope, instead, it elucidates what people can go through when there is something in their life that's not working for them, and the extent they're willing to go to fix it.

Here are some things I disliked about being fat. I hated that it was open season to talk about my weight no matter what. I hated feeling like I was defective. When you're overweight, people talk about it, to your face, all the time, especially when you're a kid, even the people that love you. Everyone wants to fix you.

I hated going to the doctor and having them stare at me, doing their best to put the fear of God in me to do something. I was ten years old, it wasn't nice or fair, there were better ways to do it.

I hated waking up feeling hungover every morning from sugar withdrawal and not even knowing that was a thing.

I hated not being able to take my shirt off. Having to sneak away to a bathroom stall to change during gym class or wearing a T-shirt while I swam. I knew people made comments, I knew they could see me, all I could do was try to hide.

I hated having to shop at stores for grown-ass men when I was twelve because nothing fit. Having to buy 3X shirts and 44-inch pants.

I hated that at thirteen I started to notice stretch marks all over my body and from that moment on, knew I'd permanently disfigured myself with hanging skin everywhere. Eventually I'd have to get my skin cut off because it would never go back on its own.

I hated knowing as an actor I could play only two parts, the best friend or the bully, because it would never be believable to be anything else. The love interest?

Nope. Superhero? Definitely not. The punch line? Yeah, that works.

I hated not going to parties. I hated not having a girl-friend.

I hated missing out on being a proper teenager.

and

I hated that the whole world could see me like this. I could go on, but you get the picture.

I don't know what is ignited in people's reptilian brains when they see someone overweight. I know at times throughout history it was thought to be a point of pride, like you could afford to eat well, but I think it may elicit an older response, not one from the Middle Ages but something earlier. I think people worry that if a lion or some sort of other predator attacks and an overweight person is around, they'll be less likely to run for safety. I'm not kidding.

Every thought I had until I was seventeen years old was preempted with *Once I lose weight I'll . . . Once I lose weight I'll get a girlfriend, Once I lose weight I'll get better roles, Once I lose weight I'll travel, Once I lose weight I'll . . .* I was in a self-imposed quarantine and I didn't feel comfortable doing anything more than hanging out with a select group of people looking like this.

I know what you're thinking. *But weren't you on television?*

Yes, I realize that's a pretty outwardly public thing to be doing when you don't want anyone to see you, but of course acting was the only thing that made me forget what I was. I would enter a flow state the moment I walked onstage, I had all the control and command of someone at ease in their body, I stopped thinking about it.

When I look back I think, *What a conflicting existence.* I was walking this fine line between getting what

I always wanted and at the same time broadsided by all the ways I was inadequate, not enough. I was living the dream and then being woken up from the dream by the public's perception of what was an acceptable appearance. In the early aughts, the standard of beauty was, to put it bluntly, not being a healthy weight but underweight. Not to mention, at that time it was open season to talk about people's weight, especially if you were funny because people thought, *Ahh, he's hilarious, he can take it!* There was a joke on the show once where I received a shirt as a gift, and upon opening the shirt it revealed that it was the size of a circus tent, to which I replied, "Is this for me or an SUV?" It's a funny joke, I love a funny joke, it just still hurt.

Imagine this. Imagine if my story up until this moment was exactly the same, but instead of acting, it was the violin. Or math or spelling, just imagine it wasn't the most public, front-facing profession possible. Mathematicians aren't supposed to be babes, chess prodigies are supposed to look like Bobby Fischer not Magnus Carlsen (Magnus is a model and also the greatest chess player alive, shout out Magnus), but actors? They're to be looked at. There are case studies that show a mouse's behavior is changed simply by being observed, the outcomes of the experiment were altered just from scientists watching it happen! Mice!

Some of you are probably thinking and with good reason, *Oh, was it hard to be loved? Was it hard to enjoy the spoils of being a recognizable person and everything that came along with it?* To be honest, as I sit here writing this,

I wonder at the validity of this whole section myself. What the fuck, reader, I thought we were friends! Look, what I think is this, obviously it was nice to have people enjoy the show. Performing for no audience is a clear sign of a madman, so yes, a large group of willing participants happy to be fed ads as they enjoy their twenty-two minutes of entertainment is integral.

Also, I suppose someone in my position, who was desperately looking for validation, might've gravitated toward a profession that supplies it in massive doses, by more than just your peers but also the general public. The greatest dentist on earth probably wouldn't mind having a few more Instagram followers. But fame, or public notoriety, the feeling of having the world become one small town because everyone knows your name also meant that everyone felt comfortable commenting on anything they deemed unsatisfactory about you. The world becomes that family member who gets drunk at Thanksgiving and tells you what they really think. World becomes small town, world also becomes drunk uncle. Kind of a wash.

Bill Murray has a quote that says, "People always say, 'I want to be rich and famous,' to which I reply, 'Why don't you try being rich first and see if that doesn't solve most of your problems?'"

My friend Teddy Purcell, the professional hockey player, always prided himself on doing what he called "the dirt work." Basically, he would hang out in front of the net, trying to deflect shots past the goalie. It wasn't glamorous, you'd constantly be taking pucks to the shin, and even if you got the goal, you didn't actually get credit for it, but somebody had to do it, and that somebody was Teddy. That's how I felt for five seasons of *Drake & Josh*, I was doing the dirt work. It wasn't pretty, I got my ass kicked sometimes, but it paid well and at least I was on the ice.

I had desperately tried to lose weight my whole life, I was probably one of the only fifteen-year-olds who was doing Keto in 2001. I tried every diet—SlimFast shakes, Atkins, Lean Cuisines—and they all worked for like a day. I could keep it up for forty-eight hours, I'd usually lose ten pounds because when you're that heavy and you restrict your diet, you lose weight quickly, but I'd be right back up the next day. It was maddening to have no self-control, no willpower. What was wrong with me? Why was I so messed up?

Saturday nights I would order a large pizza, bread-sticks, and dessert and eat the whole thing alone in my room. I'd power through it, slowly throughout the night, playing mind games, *I'm just going to have two slices and save the rest for tomorrow. I'm only going to have half, that's it, that's my last slice. I'll only eat the top of the rest, that's healthy, bread is bad for you but mozzarella cheese and pepperoni aren't, those are protein.*

It's no wonder why people's spirits get crushed, you're failing constantly.

Start a diet on Monday, cheat on Wednesday, feel bad till Sunday, start again. Over and over the cycle continues, and over and over it felt as though a little more of life was passing me by. I knew there were bigger guys who were comfortable with it, who had no problem taking their shirt off at the pool to revel a giant belly. It didn't seem to stop them from having girlfriends or lives or any of the other things that were escaping me but I was different.

Being overweight was an everyday reminder of how different I was, I was so tired of being different. I'd been different my whole life and I was sick of it. Only child, single mom–different. Overweight–different. Broke–different. Actor kid–different. I don't want it to sound ungrateful but there were times when I was sixteen, overweight, and on television that I would've traded it all to be normal, skinny, and unremarkable. Someone whose biggest problems were finals and where they were going to spend spring break.

If I got everything I wanted, if I could be the biggest movie star in the world but had to stay this weight forever, then I didn't want it.

I would've traded it all to be thin, and I couldn't waste another day of my life wishing it was different.

When I started acting, people would always compare me to other overweight actors. "Oh, you want to be like John Belushi, huh?" "You're gonna be like John Candy, I know it!" "You should watch that Chris Farley, you remind me of him." Those guys are GENIUSES, obviously, and I would be lucky to have a tenth of what they had. But people weren't comparing my talent to theirs, they were comparing my girth. It was just a snap judgment, "You're fat and want to be in movies? Hope you're funny!" And it's like it just escaped everyone's mind all these guys *died*, tragically. Young. In pain.

Out of the blue in 2002, I booked a role that gave me a peek into what it could feel like to play a real person.

Mean Creek was an independent film directed by Jacob Aaron Estes about a group of kids who invite their local bully on a boat trip to prank and humiliate him, only to have it result in disaster. I played the terroristic bully who, by the second act of the film, reveals how misunderstood he is, how his learning disability affects his interactions with people, and how desperately he wanted friends. My character, George Tooney, was heartbreaking, and it was the first time I ever got to play someone so painfully flawed, someone who couldn't get out of their own way, someone so human.

I knew what it meant to have people make a snap judgment about you from your appearance. I knew what it meant to sit at home in your room, dreaming about being normal, and hanging out with other kids. I gave George every moment of my life until that point, every feeling, and he was a fully realized character because of it. He was real.

The reaction to the movie was stellar. It won the Americana Award at the Sundance Film Festival and I got to give the acceptance speech at the Independent Spirit Awards, where we won the Special Distinction Award. I was floored by people's reaction, especially by my performance. I think that on *Drake & Josh* people always assumed the character was just an exaggerated version of me, I mean we shared the same name. No one knew I was capable of going to this place. But I knew, and I wanted more of it.

I wasn't going to wait another ten years for this kind of part to come around again. There wasn't a Jonah Hill or Paul Hauser or Seth Rogen to look up to, guys doing cool, interesting parts while also not being the typical leading man type. If I wanted to play these parts, then I needed to be able to transform, and I couldn't do that at the weight I was at.

If you're shaking your head at that last paragraph, I get it. Maybe it was an excuse, maybe I could have made it at the size I was, I just had to work a little harder and be a little better. But I think I also needed to feel free. In my mind I had built up losing weight for so long I needed to see what life felt like in that body. I just couldn't let my guard down, as an actor or as a person, until it happened.

That movie, that conversation with my mom, along with wanting this every second of my life until this point, made me ready. I was seventeen and I was prepared to do the thing that had eluded me my entire life. People tried to warn me, "Ya know, people tend to not be as funny after they lose weight," or, "Aren't you worried about what the audience's reaction will be if you lose weight?"

I. DIDN'T. CARE.

When someone asks for weight-loss advice, I wish I had a better answer than "Ya know, just diet and exercise" because I KNOW how badly they want some hack, some secret to help with what feels like an impossible task, I know

I did. But that's how I did it. From that day in the car and every day forward, I ate a little less and worked out a little more, for eighteen months, until I lost 120 pounds.

I did the basics, tried to limit carbs, tried to limit sugar, tried to eat more protein, but when I messed up, I didn't go into a shame spiral for weeks eating everything in sight. I just started again, live to fight another day, I thought. When I plateaued, I tightened my diet. But when it came to working out? Well, that was more complicated.

At first I just walked, that's all I could do, it was the only thing that didn't hurt. I'd throw on headphones and walk nonstop. *Just stay moving, dream of what your life's going to be like,* I thought. After a while I was willing to get into the gym but it was with great reticence considering every experience I'd had with fitness was humiliating and this was no different.

I started to begrudgingly show up a few times a week with a trainer, who would literally wrap a towel around my waist, like I was an injured whale, and LIFT me as I struggled to do a single push-up... from my knees. I had never done a push-up before. I mean I had a childhood, kind of, I remember going to gym class, but somewhere along the way I had avoided push-ups. Same goes for pull-ups, sit-ups, and any other sort of ups. The entire gym would root me on like a kid with no limbs in a footrace, it was kind of them but also supremely embarrassing. I didn't let it deter me, I went every day and slowly I got better, one push-up at a time.

Days became weeks, weeks turned into months of working out and eating right, and after eighteen months I had done it. I got to my goal weight of 180 pounds. I would go to stores and buy every piece of clothing I was too embarrassed to wear before, I would try to run into people I hadn't seen in years just to hear them say, "Oh my God!" It wasn't perfect, but I did feel better.

The weirdest part of all of this, though, was that this whole weight-loss experience was documented on television. I went from a gigantically large sixteen-year-old to a fairly human-size eighteen-year-old over the two final seasons of *Drake & Josh* and people didn't know how to handle it. I mean it's weird and rare to watch someone lose that much weight in real life, but when it's someone you're used to seeing on television, it's even weirder. The whole world was part of my weight-loss journey whether I liked it or not, and people wanted answers.

Suddenly I was bombarded with questions: "You a sleeve guy? You get the surgery where they make your stomach the size of an egg? Adderall? You took Adderall, right?" to *People* magazine asking me to be on their cover. Magazines, talk shows, and more all wanted to feature me to talk about my big transformation.

Even more surprising was the backlash, the anger people had about me losing weight. People tend to marry themselves to the first image they have of you. Ever had a parent or grandparent say, "You'll always be my little boy [or girl]"?

Ya, same thing. People have an idealized picture of you, they want you to be the thing you were before they got to know you, before they found faults, before you had a mind of your own. For the world that was me as an overweight teen but suddenly that image was gone. I had taken it from them, someone they loved, and they didn't like it. Comments were slung at me such as "You were funnier when you were fat!" and "Stop trying so hard!" Me losing weight held a mirror to the people who watched me, forcing them to watch someone change in real time and consider their own growth and change. Not everyone likes being forced to reflect.

Meanwhile, I just wanted people to forget it ever happened. Who among us wants to revisit our high school years and regale in the memories of cystic acne and neverending nosebleeds? Not me! I mean the compliments were nice, but all I wanted, all I ever wanted was to be considered a REAL actor, not a child actor, not a funny fat guy, and certainly not a poster boy for Weight Watchers.

For those reasons, I've never really talked about my weight loss except to make fun of it. I look back at old pictures of me, old episodes of the show, and think, *Who is that guy?* It took me a really long time to make peace with him. With the fact that this was always going to be a permanent chapter, I couldn't rewrite my origin story. I hated that guy for a really long time, fat Josh. Why couldn't he just control himself? Why'd he have to embarrass us like that and destroy our body? I know it's weird to talk about it in the third person, but again, it's like he was a different person.

It took me a really long time to love that kid, to realize that without him there would be no me. I was scared, powerless, and alone, and he protected me against an intense and unrelenting existence. I appreciate that kid, I don't judge him anymore, he was strong in a way that I no longer have to be, and had he not done what he did, I might not be here today. Okay, enough third-person talk, it's weirding me out.

I realize now that instead of people forgetting about young Josh, I had become this reluctant inspiration to people experiencing their own weight-loss journey and they deserved more than just a joke about it. Getting in shape for me was a selfish endeavor, something I would've done regardless of whether or not I was in the public eye, but that didn't matter. Just because I intended one thing doesn't change reality, the results were something different, and I had to act accordingly.

Show business is weird, it attracts some of the most self-serving, self-obsessed, self-centric people on earth whose sole purpose is accruing as much fame and financial prestige as possible, and yet I now know there is a virtuous aspect to what we are trying to do. Hopefully, when done right, movies and television can serve as reprieves for people watching them. People with real jobs, real worries, real stakes can escape from the reality of their world for a few hours and lose themselves in our world, the one we create. And if you can inspire on top of it, motivate someone to change for the better, well now it's more than that. It's some Oprah shit.

What was more important than my comfort, or my desire to rewrite history, was that people approached me regularly and said, "You inspired me to get in shape" or "My son is struggling with weight loss. Can you give him any advice?"

So here goes. To anyone in the fight, to anyone still struggling the way I did for so long, this is what I want to say, "When you're ready, you'll do it." What changed for me was that I was thoroughly convinced that my way didn't work anymore, and if I didn't take action, I might never take it. No amount of evidence could've persuaded me to do it a second sooner. I had to exhaust all options, I had to be miserable. So if you too are miserable, sick of it, frustrated, overwhelmed, and utterly over it, you might just be in a very good place to start.

I wish I could say losing 120 pounds made me all better, but you knew it wouldn't, I mean, we're only halfway through the book. An odd thing happened after I got down to my goal weight. It seems as though those critical voices, that anger that swam through my head, the crippling self-obsession were all muted by this whirlwind of a journey I was on. I was riding high from the promise of a new life I was beginning. But as soon as I was done, as soon as I had arrived, I started hearing whispers again, those old familiar feelings started creeping back. I needed something to take care of it, something new, something better.

9

When Existing Is Exhausting

Every night since that bathroom with Jessica, every single night since that night when I looked up at her and said yes to my first dose of real drugs, I was not sober.

For four years I didn't take a sober breath except the time between waking up and locating whatever mind-altering substance was closest. Not when I was with Ben Kingsley, not when I was around my mom, not even when I was on screen. Usually weed, and then pills, and then infinity. I never began the day with the intention to do hard drugs, but once my resistance was weakened by that first hit, it always ended in the same place. I would do whatever would pack the biggest punch to get me as close to not here as possible.

Drugs and alcohol were the greatest baits and switches of my life, and if I'm being honest, they were fun for only a few weeks. The repercussions of my recreational drug use started to pile up rapidly, which is probably because

I didn't do them recreationally, I did them professionally. My using quickly devolved from the normal, get high and go to a party with a bunch of people, to get high with a bunch of people who want to sit in a room and get high.

I broke off from that crew of kids who introduced me to this world and found new people who liked to drink and use the way I did. People with names such as The Professor and White Mike and a *Sesame Street* character I won't name because he might kill me. This group of beatnik degenerates' sole purpose was getting high, they didn't need to dress it up with a DJ booth and dance floor, they were the sordid underbelly of a really weird world and . . . I liked it.

Within months of my first time, I found myself using in crappy apartments and bombed-out minivans with people such as Willie, who was on the run for stealing a rental car, Gabe, who until recently had been a lawyer but was disbarred for being high in court, and Eve, who was studying fashion downtown while also balancing her crack habit, which made her face look like it was falling off.

Good times!

I don't know how I'm making these people sound, because I want to make it clear—I am also them. As in, they weren't bad people, they were broken people. These were my compatriots, my suppliers of good times and misfortune. I felt more comfortable with them than anyone else I'd ever hung out with.

Why?

Here's the thing, drug addicts hanging out together is

like a self-help group without the help. The kind of drugs we did, the way we did them, meant we were all running from something bad, something deep within us implanted from birth or from circumstance but whatever it was, it was enough for us to revolve our whole world around getting and staying high. Gabe being a lawyer, Eve being a student, me being a child actor, these were our part-time jobs, our main job was to chase that feeling that drugs gave us, that relief, that vacation from self.

I'll never forget arriving at some apartment in the valley, Eve or Gabe or Willie waiting for me, and the collective breath we took as we began to feel the effects of whatever intoxicant we'd just ingested. The crack of a lighter, the sound of an inhale, and oblivion. We'd look at each other, in this collective moment of bliss, with this unspoken feeling, like the crew of a ship who made it through an impossible storm. But we weren't just the crew, we were also the storm.

I guess if when you're born, your default settings are at odds with the world around you, if the daily task of just existing is exhausting and you find some relief in drugs and alcohol, it's no wonder why you would sit at the altar of it for as long and as hard as you could.

Food had been sort of killing me softly. It was a slow, patient force—happy to wait decades before it wiped me off the face of the earth, but drugs were different. Their efficacy was so much stronger, which also meant their consequences were that much stronger. When I traded food for drugs, it seemed as though everything sped up dramatically.

It was like trading a Prius for a Ferrari with no brakes, you'll get to where you're headed faster but there's a good chance if you keep going that speed you'll die in the process.

My whole life, I romanticized drug addicts. Hunter S. Thompson, Basquiat, Bourdain, Burrows, and other guys whose name starts in B because they didn't give a fuck and all I did was give a fuck. All I cared about was what you thought and what the world thought about me and it was all wrapped up in my livelihood. I hope this casting director likes me so I get this job, so I can make enough money to get me and my mom out of here, and I hope you like the job I do so I can get another job, because I can't survive off one job, and I hope you don't think poorly of me because I'm the size of a house, because I think poorly of me and I wouldn't blame you.

Whatever happened in that bathroom that night changed me, relieved me of old Josh. He was gone. I was going to MAKE you forget him. Any positive feeling you had about him had to be erased because I hated that guy. This was the real me, the Josh I was always meant to be, an eyes sunken, underweight, unreliable mess.

So yeah, my life began to crash and burn fast. Need some examples?

There was running from the police in front of the Beverly Hills Hotel, of course. But that was just the beginning.

At nineteen, after a particularly hard-charging weekend of treating my body like a chemistry set, I showed up to work at 6:00 a.m., having not slept since Saturday, walked onto the set, and collapsed in front of a hundred of my co-workers. I didn't smell toast, my life didn't flash before my eyes, it was just one moment I was here, the next I wasn't. My body overruled and said that we needed a hard reset. I woke up in the arms of one of the assistant directors and a swarm of worried onlookers all asking me if I needed an ambulance. I didn't need an ambulance, I needed an anti-depressant and a Gatorade, I needed a father figure and a year off. I tried to reassure them that it was simply low blood sugar but they knew, they'd seen me spiraling for months.

In 2006, right as I had finished filming *Drake & Josh*, I booked a big film with a big comedy team, one who really appreciated the powers of a funny Jew such as myself . . . and I completely squandered the opportunity. I showed up late, was less than professional when it came to my preparation, and inevitably was just a liability. I received this email from the producer of the film on a day when I came especially late and kept production waiting for more than an hour. This email is mostly from memory because it was fifteen years ago, and I'm not sure I have access to the AOL account—MrMoney86—anymore. I promise you though, I couldn't forget this email if I tried.

Josh,

When you're late, it slows up the entire production, everyone is waiting on you, and it pushes us to have to go into overtime, which costs the production money we don't have. I understand this is not the first time you've been late and that will never work for this production or any other. You're killing it when it comes to the comedy, but your professionalism needs work. . . .

I've omitted the rest of the note, but you get the picture.

By the way, the producer who wrote me that email? His name is Judd Apatow. I shanked the opportunity that could have changed my life. I said earlier that when I was younger there weren't roles for offbeat leading men like Seth Rogen or Jonah Hill. But Judd Apatow is the guy who made that possible. Judd couldn't have been cooler, he took a shot on me and I ruined it. I was a drug addict who couldn't get it together long enough to show up for my responsibilities. I've told him this to his face but I'm still incredibly sorry fifteen years later. It haunts me in my house, one tenth the size that it could have been had I not shot my career in the face.

One summer night in 2006, my mom showed up at my apartment after being tipped off by a few dubious confidants of mine and tried to take me to rehab. After spending hours convincing her that I was fine, that these "friends" were just overreacting and this was merely a bad weekend, she gave in. Once she left, I proceeded to hate-ingest everything and anything left in my apartment that could remotely trigger a head change. This wasn't the first or the last time my mom would try to save me, I don't think she slept for four years, it hurts to even write that.

It takes a lot of strength to stay in the emotional orbit of an addict. You have to sit there and accept being radiated while the addict becomes nuclear. The great lie most of us tell ourselves is that we're the only one being hurt by our actions and choices, but in my experience that couldn't be further from the truth. You hurt everyone who has the guts to go on loving you, and eventually their only option is to walk away, no matter how much they want to help.

And here you were thinking that drugs were exciting and sexy when in fact they were like an aboveground pool, great in theory, terrible in practice.

At about this time, something very peculiar happened. Despite proving to one of the biggest producers in Hollywood that I was basically Charlie Sheen with less talent, despite spending most of my days dumping chemicals into my body like I was a pool in need of cleaning, I attracted one of the biggest roles of my life. A part so perfectly suited for me, that it was as though everything over the last few years had prepared me for this moment. It was that role I referenced earlier playing a drug dealer opposite Ben Kingsley in the film *The Wackness*. At the height of my addiction, I secured this life-changing role for myself, I don't know how except for the fact that I literally was this character.

Every day until the first day of shooting, I wasn't sober, but for the entire six-week shoot, I was. I was scared straight, terrified to blow a role opposite my hero. I worked hard, I showed up on time, and I gained the respect of my peers. I did a good job in the film and I knew it, it was nice to feel proud, I hadn't felt that in a while.

I liked this Josh, and so did everyone I worked with, but he vanished the moment the movie was over. The second we stopped filming, it was back on, like I'd never missed a beat, *that was a cute vacation, now let's get back to what we really do.* It was like my habit had been waiting patiently for me, knowing at the right time it would have me back, it always got me back. Because for me, home is where the medicine is, whether it's sitting in my room with a pizza, or in some apartment with a buffet of mind-altering substances, I needed to be sufficiently numbed.

When I got home from filming, the next few months were markedly unremarkable. They weren't my best but they weren't my worst either, by now I was well into the fourth year of using, and I was basically just maintaining. Maybe "functioning" is a better word. I was functioning, it wasn't pretty, but I was getting by, figuring out how to balance my habit with the least amount of wreckage possible.

In hindsight, though, I could see something was changing, I remember a wave of sadness coming over me—partly because I'd just had this incredible experience filming for two months but mostly because the illusion was starting to wear off. Throughout my life, anything and everything I've ever used to quiet my mind, to not *feel*, has eventually stopped working. It's like that piece of clothing you just had to buy that's now in the donation pile, and if you stop long enough to look at it you have to face what made you buy that thing in the first place. The synapses in my brain were wearing out, the receptors stopped receiving, and I had to have something else, something better, stronger. It happened when I traded food for drugs, but what was stronger than that?

Fame. Fame might fix me.

The Wackness got into the Sundance Film Festival and all of a sudden that sadness I had been feeling for the past few months evaporated. I realize this is far from an Oscar, but for me it was an incredibly exciting moment. I attended the festival when I was sixteen, I had a small part in a movie called *Spun*, and I remember thinking, *One day, I'm going to come back here as the star of a movie.* That's exactly what I did.

Sundance in the mid-2000s was the apex of indie film-making, there was a buzz in the air, an electricity. People's lives would change in an instant when their movie would screen in front of an audience of Hollywood elite, and financiers. The moment the lights came up, they would either be bombarded with offers to buy their film for millions, or maybe there were no offers and they were left to contemplate their life choices. It was so easy to become intoxicated by the amount of potential in the air, your life could change in an instant, and I was ready for that to happen. Maybe this would fix me.

I arrived in Park City, Utah, along with the filmmakers

and we were the toast of the festival. The early buzz on the film was really good, we got a prime spot in the biggest theater at Sundance, the Eccles, which holds twelve hundred people, Quentin Tarantino was at the premiere, and most importantly, my hero Sir Ben Kingsley was there. As the credits began to roll, the lights came up and I heard this roar of applause, and after another moment, my manager whispered, "They're standing." I turned around and saw fifteen hundred people on their feet, applauding what we had made. It was like fifteen hundred fathers all telling me how proud they were.

The movie sold in an instant, the reviews were incredible, and I just wanted to get the hell out of there.

But why, Josh, why?!

Can't you just enjoy this, Jesus, can't you enjoy ANYTHING?! I know, I know dear reader, it must be exhausting to read, can you imagine what it was like to live it? I have been on a quest my entire life to find contentment through the outside world and now at my professional apex I was as miserable as I'd ever been? I know, I know.

I just didn't feel like I deserved any of it, I didn't feel like I belonged there, I don't know why other than the famous quote "I'd never want to be a part of any club that would have me as a member." Now that they wanted me, I was suspicious of the whole enterprise.

Fame wouldn't fix me, either. I finally had empirical evidence. At this once-in-a- lifetime moment my mind was still getting the better of me. My worst fear, a suspicion

I'd had my entire life, was realized. If you spend the bulk of your life looking for a reprieve from self, a mental off switch, some kind of spiritual circuit breaker to just shut the whole thing down for a minute, you'll find yourself fiercely dedicated to the R & D of the easy fix. Food? Medium effectiveness but with negative side effects. Drugs? Insanely efficacious but with side effects such as death or imprisonment. Sex, gambling, spending, cutting, bad relationships, eating disorders, smoking, hoarding, all in my opinion runners-up but certainly worth mentioning.

Our minds are the original supercomputers, an electric box full of neurons and blood vessels acting as the 1s and 0s necessary to keep YOU OS going. But what happens if your computer is corrupted? What happens if the programming is wrong? Well, that presents a problem. You could try buying your computer a new case, you could get it a really fancy printer to keep it company, you could try updating it, but unless you actually go in there and fix that bad coding it'll never work. It'll look nice, but there will always be a misfire, a glitch, an error.

That's what was happening for me after spending my entire life under the delusion that once I achieved some version of utopia, then and only then would I feel happy. I didn't feel like I belonged there, but more importantly I didn't feel like I belonged anywhere, and that was the scariest part. The promise of someday I'll feel better kept me going but if I no longer had that, well then, why keep going?

The sobering reality of all this was too much to handle,

and I certainly didn't want to have this emotional epiphany in Utah. As I packed my bag, frantically asking my manager's assistant to "book me a flight, any flight, I just gotta get out of here," people screamed at me, "You're leaving?! Why?? You have a hit movie at the festival, stay and enjoy it, it may never happen again!" I didn't care, I wanted the safety of home, where the drug laws were more forgiving. Shout out California and their lackluster drug legislation.

Peter Travers, the film critic for *Rolling Stone* and a powerful voice in film, wanted to interview me right before I left. This was a great honor, Peter is one of the smartest, most insightful reviewers, and if he loved your film, a lot of people would know about it. I remember showing up, the snow-kissed mountains planted perfectly behind Peter, and beginning the interview. It was all going well until, a few minutes in, a producer stopped us.

"What's going on?" Peter asked.

"Peter, I'm so sorry to tell you this, but Heath Ledger just died."

A collective gasp traveled across the room, publicists rushed to their Blackberries, people started welling up, total shock.

Brad Renfro, another extremely talented actor, also had died that week. Both of a drug overdose.

I didn't know either of these guys other than being a huge fan of them both, but something struck me about their passing. It was weird to see the effect it had on people who didn't even know them personally and yet were so hurt by them passing. It made the effects, the sobering reality of the impact we have on people real, the heartbreak, the loss.

I looked up to those guys, they weren't much older than I was.

They say alcoholics respond well to catastrophe, that a DUI, or their wife leaving, or a bad health diagnosis can wake them up if only for a moment, and within that window they have their best chance of getting sober. If an alcoholic calls you for help and is ready to stop drinking, don't let them take a nap because they might wake up and think, *Meh, it wasn't THAT bad.*

That's where I was when I got home.

I was at a crossroads and the universe allowed me to see that. My life wasn't in complete shambles, not yet, but it was a far cry morally and spiritually from who I was as a person. I knew that if I didn't take some action, I would default to my old ways and the cycle would continue until it wasn't my morals I was worried about, but my freedom.

There were too many close calls, too many rides across the lawn of the Beverly Hills Hotel, too many trips to the ER, where I convinced them it was anxiety making my heart do that. Too many times there should have been a picture of me on TMZ, instead of literally outing myself in this book for some reason.

My luck was running out.

10

Laugh Loud, Cry Hard

I've been going to twelve-step meetings since I was six years old.

My mom became a member of Alcoholics Anonymous and Overeaters Anonymous when she was twenty-eight, she has remained mostly sober since then and has never stopped attending meetings, so naturally when she gave birth to me, I went there too. From the age of six till I was old enough to stay alone, I was sitting in meetings, playing GameBoy, and counting the minutes till it was over. I didn't mind it, the cookies were good, the people were nice, I just didn't understand why we had to frequent so many church basements.

Growing up around the twelve steps meant recovery wasn't foreign to me. I knew the serenity prayer before I knew algebra. My mom's closest friends were the people from her meetings and they were these beautiful characters who always wanted to eat Chinese food. One guy even took me to a Mets game and another to the United

Nations, where he worked as a cameraman. I was directly affected by the sober community in a really positive way.

None of that mattered when it was my turn to get sober, of course.

The Greek philosopher Heraclitus said, "No man ever steps in the same river twice, for it's not the same river and **he's not the same man**." At no point as I lay wide awake, heart beating out of my chest, and watching the sun come up did I think, *Maybe I should give AA a try.*

I do remember once, though, in the midst of my using and drinking, sitting in a meeting with my mom (she'd sometimes trick me into going with her when I would show up at her house particularly beat up) and thinking, *I'll probably end up here one day but not now.* Even through the haze of my using, there was some part of my brain still abovewater telling me, *We can't really go on like this, can we, Josh?*

When I got home from Sundance I did what any respectable addict would do on the precipice of recovery: I tried to drink the problem away. Sure, I'd just been shaken awake from a nightmare, alerted by the gods that there was no way I could go on like this, but I might as well give NOT doing it a shot too, right? The unknown is scary, and I was used to this life, I mean I didn't like it but there's something to be said for being used to something. I was like a fighter pilot with a broken plane, sure the cabin's on fire but this is a good plane! It took me to a lot of places and what happens when I hit the eject button? Unfortunately, all of my attempts didn't work. I doubled my dose, tried changing medicines, but the result was the same, I couldn't forget what I saw. I tried to numb my brain to the realization that I had but it was futile, I was high and miserable—the worst combination. It's a very scary moment for a drug addict when they can't get high anymore and they can't get sober, because there're only two options left, chase death or chase life.

When people find out my sobriety date is February 15 they always ask, "What happened on Valentine's Day?" As though I were in any position to be someone's Valentine at that time in my life. Let me give you a snapshot of what my life looked like on February 14, 2008.

I was underweight, with gigantic circles around my eyes and translucent skin. My body hurt and I would sometimes break out in a flop sweat for no reason. I would shake, I would shake a lot, like if I had to hold a cup or write my name, it looked like my hand was on a Tilt-A-Whirl, people asked if I had a degenerative nerve issue, I told them it was low blood sugar. I'd had multiple trips to the Emergency Room because of "anxiety" but mostly because I was afraid I had taken too much of something and thought I might die. Oh, and I had this pesky staph infection in my arm that didn't want to heal.

I had started to repulse almost everyone who cared about me and was running out of people who could even stand to be around me. I was blowing through what little money I had left. I was constantly one traffic stop away from being arrested, and at work I was getting the reputation of being unreliable, unprofessional, and unhinged. I'd show up looking bad or not at all and get random calls from friends saying, "Hey dude, are you good?"

One night in North Hollywood, I picked up pills from a guy in an apartment, and then left my car parked on the street while I went to meet a buddy to eat the pills and grab some food. An hour later I walked back to three or four police cars parked out front and caution tape wrapped around the whole building as the guy who sold me the pills was being carted out on a gurney. Someone got hip to the pill guy's operation and decided to show up at his house with a knife and see what happened. Both of them got very stabbed and very arrested in the process and it all happened ten minutes after I left.

There were many close calls. Could I have pushed it further? Of course. Unless you're locked up or six feet under, there's always room to make things worse. But I had also been inside my own head since I could form memories, and knew this wasn't just a phase. I had been wrestling with this feeling my whole life and I was losing. Plus I wasn't anonymous, so the first time I got arrested or caught up, it would've come with so much more attention than for your normal first-time offender. I didn't know how to navigate the world with or without drugs, but I knew with them I wouldn't have a world to navigate much longer.

So on February 15, 2008, three weeks after Sundance, I walked into a meeting of Alcoholics Anonymous for the first time on my own accord, not because I was too young to stay alone, not to make my mom happy—but because I was broken and I knew I needed help. I didn't know if they had the kind of help I needed, but it was the only place I knew to go.

I found a chair leaning against a wall, the smells of burned coffee and linoleum floors wafting through the air, folding chairs set up in rows, the lack of air-conditioning. I sat off to the side taking in this scene, this secret headquarters of misfits, grifters, and thieves.

In reality, it was a 3:00 p.m. meeting at a church in North Hollywood, so for the most part everyone looked like they'd just left a Costco. There were more cargo shorts and sandals than high heels, and combat boots. The room was full of men and women young and old, of all ethnicities and backgrounds, some beat up, some well kept, it seemed addiction was an equal opportunity offender.

I watched from the safety of my seat as people laughed, hugged, smoked, and stood in line for coffee that looked like motor oil. There were bikers, homeless dudes, people younger than I was, and women who looked like they wore their best outfits. Most people had teeth, some did not, but everyone seemed, for the most part, comfortable.

The meeting began, a guy holding a giant-size coffee called out, "Hi, I'm Rick and I'm an alcoholic." And then on cue in unison, the entire room erupted in a "Hi, Rick."

There was some housekeeping, "Please make sure you don't block the priest's car in the parking lot," along with some guidelines, "Feel free to use any kind of language during the meeting but when on church grounds, try to keep the cursing to a minimum, we're freaking out the fucking church members." People took plastic chips for thirty, sixty, and ninety days of sobriety, they got a hug and a big round of applause as they announced how long they had. "Hi, I'm Natalia, I'm an alcoholic, and I have thirty-eight days."

It was all fairly civilized, but far from special. I was waiting for the secret sauce, what was this thing that had helped so many? Because if this was just a social club for people who chain-smoked and ingested too much caffeine, I wasn't interested.

And then I heard, "And now for our speaker, please welcome Kevin," and in that moment, something changed. Kevin shared his story of getting sober and it was like hearing an orchestra go from warming up to full volume. Much like the first time I did drugs, it was as though a frequency began to be broadcast, one that my internal radio was perfectly tuned to hear. Other people began to share their stories too, they talked about the way they liked to drink and use and how different it was than their fellows. They recalled stories of their spectacular antics while loaded, stories that would probably scare most people but here were met with laughter and nods of identification.

They talked about how wonderfully insufferable the

task of living could be, how their lives could be punctuated at any moment by utter defeat, fear, and anxiety. But as quick as they were to spout off about the trappings of existence, they were just as quick to talk about the deep gratitude for the new life they'd been given, the families and relationships that had been restored, and their appreciation for even the smallest moments. These were fallible people doing their best to get through life and conceding to the idea that they needed help. Revelatory.

I had never heard people speak like this. Obviously not when I was seven, focusing more on my GameBoy than what was going on in the meeting I had been dragged to, but not in my adult life either. Aren't grown-ups supposed to have it all figured out? When you're a kid that's the assumption and you really don't begin to see the cracks till later. I remember a buddy whose family life seemed like the picture of normalcy, his parents were great, their snack drawer was full, and he always had new games for Xbox. It wasn't till later I realized his father got high and slept on the couch every night and his mom drank a bottle of wine when she watched us.

I sat in that meeting and what happened next is best described by using a quote from a sober friend who said it better than I ever could, "You didn't tell me what was wrong with ME, you told me what was wrong with YOU and I identified." That's about as good an explanation as I've ever heard. The people in that room told my story by telling theirs. They thought too much, drank too much, felt too deeply, and hurt too many.

What I'm going to say next is one of the biggest capital T truths of who I am, and I feel like by this point, we're close enough to go there. You've got my heart, dear reader, don't break it. The TRUTH is, I have walked around my entire life feeling terminally unique. That God or evolution or whatever you believe in glitched when I was being cooked. I'm like a cake that was taken out of the oven too early, normal to the naked eye but mush the moment you cut into it. I'd read self-help books and studied psychology doing my best to find some diagnosis for the way I felt. Depression? Sure I had some of that, Anxiety? You better believe it. All-or-nothing thinking, obsessive thoughts, throw those in too. What do I win, Bob?! A one-way trip to the mental hospital, Josh!

However, none of those things encapsulated me, and it would be a disservice to those truly suffering to label myself as that. But the way these people talked? Oh yeah, that was me. I was being diagnosed, and for the first time ever, I wasn't alone, there was a word for people like me, and it was "alcoholic." Fuck.

I sat taking it all in, I had been beaten into a state of willingness from four years of abuse and a lifetime of discomfort. I was tired, tired enough to listen when I heard people say, "If you're here, it means your best thinking got you a front-row seat in Alcoholics Anonymous," or

"Give it ninety days, if it doesn't work, we'll refund your misery."

On that day, at that moment, I was ready. The meeting ended and people started to file out, I was shaken, I didn't know what to do with myself.

I got up to leave just as this man approached and said, "Ya new, kid?" He was in his mid-fifties with a short haircut and surely looked like he had done some professional drinking in his day. He had deep crinkles around his eyes that were noticeable when he smiled, which was often. I remember once he told me, "Josh, I laugh louder and cry harder than most people, I guess that's just what happens when you've lived." This was my first sponsor, Marvin. I answered him in what could have only been a whisper, "Um yeah, I'm new" to which he replied "That's fantastic."

We chatted more, general stuff, he worked as a teamster in the movie business, made sense, he had the air of a guy in a union—I told him I was an actor, he said he hadn't heard of me, ya know, getting-to-know-you stuff. I knew I needed this thing called a "sponsor" and figured if there was anyone I could muster up the courage to ask, it was him. Asking someone to be your sponsor is much like asking someone to be your prom date, it's a huge deal in the moment, but the reality is you probably won't talk to them in ten years.

We walked to our cars and I blurted out, "Hey would you like, want to be my sponsor?" He looked at me with a half smile, "Tell ya what, meet me at this meeting tonight at eight, then we can talk about it." Yikes, two meetings in one day? I'm messed up, but I'm not THAT messed up. I think in hindsight, he just wanted to see if I was willing to take even the smallest direction, to see if I was serious. I showed up at that meeting, Marvin saved me a seat, and afterward he said, "You like Italian food?"

We sat in the back booth of an Italian restaurant in a strip mall, it was the kind of place you go when you're not welcome at other establishments. Marvin ordered garlic bread and a side of marinara sauce as his main dish, which I of course found odd because it is so clearly an appetizer. I ordered the chicken cacciatore because while all psychoactive substances had a season pass to my body, carbs did not.

I sat there for the next two hours and told him my entire life story, unedited.

Everything bad that had ever happened to me, the dad that didn't want me, the money we didn't have, the weight I couldn't lose, the responsibility of supporting a family at fifteen, and all the other reasons why I felt justified in going on this four-year vision quest. He sat there, dunking his bread in marinara sauce, letting me talk, nodding, listening, nodding. In hindsight, I realize that I probably wasn't the first guy he had taken to this restaurant to hear their life story, and he'd developed a system that would allow him to eat unlimited amounts of garlic bread as he listened.

After dinner, Marvin told me to call him the next day

and we'd go to another meeting. That was it, my assignment, go to a meeting the next day.

My head was swimming as I left the restaurant, I was overwhelmed both by what I'd heard and what I'd said, but I knew one thing without a shadow of a doubt: I was an alcoholic. Now, for most I would imagine this classification might be a shameful one, "Oh God, not me, I can't be one of THOSE people, that moniker is reserved for the lowest of the lows, the MOST desperate" when in reality, finally discovering what I was, was the most freeing moment of my life. Because these people like Marvin, who identified as alcoholics, weren't shattered, they weren't social outcasts, they were fully evolved people, joyous and grateful. They seemed to have all the cash and prizes that came with a good life.

I would come to learn that I would never have a normal relationship with alcohol and drugs. "Surrender to win," they told me. I never had to manage my drinking or survive another hangover again, I'd tried my best to drink like a gentleman, to be the cool, creative type who got recreationally high, but it didn't work. I had lost the war but I was on the wrong side of it. It was like I'd spent my entire life trying to reason with a peanut allergy, maybe if I just eat half a peanut butter cup I'll be fine. NO! Move on to an alternate nut, my friend, because you do not mix well with these peanuts. A buddy said once, "You're a pickle, you'll never be a cucumber again and as long as you know that, you'll be fine. Plus, people love pickles."

I met Marvin at a meeting the next day, and the next day after that. I went to one every day for months, I didn't have anything else to do, and well, I didn't have anything else to do. I became friends with other people my age who were getting sober, some with more time than I had, some with less, it felt good to have friends who weren't doing typical twenty-year-old things. We'd go to late-night meetings followed by all-night diners, where we'd eat pie and trade stories till we were so buzzed on sugar, the only place we wanted to go was bed. Another day sober, put it in the bank.

I was riding the pink cloud of sobriety. For the first time in years my body didn't have any intoxicants in it, so obviously I felt better, but more than that, I felt hopeful. I finally felt I could live under the social contract my peers were living by, that I could operate in the world that is, instead of the world I thought I deserved. I was healing.

About six months into sobriety, it was suggested I attend an all-men AA meeting. This scared me because the moment I heard all-men anything, I assumed I didn't possess the requisite testosterone to qualify. I had become better and better at taking suggestions over the past few months, though, and what awaited me, it turns out, was exactly what I needed.

I walked into this room, and there was an electricity to it. These were guys from all walks of life, mostly older and with a lot of time sober, there was even a World War Two vet with almost sixty years. Every Monday and Thursday night, eighty guys would assemble in the side room of a church, and for ninety minutes they would have one hell of an AA meeting. The meeting had sort of an unofficial structure, the young guys with less time were encouraged to share first, what they were going though, any problems they might have, and as the meeting progressed those same guys were encouraged to shut up and listen to what the older ones had to say.

It wasn't a hierarchy, like I have more status than you because I've been sober longer, it was that many of the people in that room had walked through similar situations and stayed sober. That's it. Here, let me help you, I've summited this peak before, and these are the holds. It wasn't advice, it was perspective. The problems ranged from "How do I tell this girl I've been dating I don't drink" to "I'm facing jail time for something I did while I was using, and I don't know what to do." No matter what the problem, though, the answer always seemed to entail these three things:

Do it scared.

Do the right thing, especially when no one's watching. Be in the efforts business, not the results.

Face the judge, face the girl, face the problem head on. No more running.

A guy once said, "You can do anything you want in sobriety as long as you're willing to face the consequences." The idea was that the discomfort associated with having to lie, hide, and cheat your way through life was liable to make you drink again, so clean up your past even if it means turning yourself in. I'd also seen members of that group write letters to a judge expressing the change they'd seen in a guy facing a jail sentence and asking for some leniency. It almost always worked.

The kind of insight that came out of that room probably sounds basic to some, but for me, it was a revelation. When guys would share that they had low self-esteem, the response was naturally "Do estimable acts." When someone said they couldn't get out of their own head, the response was "Help someone and you won't have time to think about yourself." If someone lamented about their wife or girlfriend, the response was "Bring her in next week so we can hear her side."

It wasn't that people didn't have legitimate gripes, it was that they were irrelevant. If we're not the problem, then there could be no solution. We couldn't control the outside world, the wife, the employer, the judge who took issue with us, we could only control our perspective on it and how we chose to react. And the best response, more times than not, was no reaction at all.

Don't get me wrong, it wasn't always spiritual nirvana, I had seen more than a few guys storm out of there after someone blurted out "waaaaaaaa" in the middle of their share. It wasn't for everyone, there were plenty of meetings for people who needed a shoulder to cry on, but this wasn't one of them. The only thing they were concerned about was not drinking and helping the next guy. Get better, then help someone else get better.

Over time I became part of that group. Stay close to the pack, they said, it's the ones on the outside who get picked off. I got a commitment cleaning the coffeepots, and it became a big point of pride to thoroughly wash them each week. I was contributing, I was gaining the respect of these guys I looked up to. At any moment someone might turn to you and say, "When's your sobriety date, kid?" "February fifteenth," I'd reply. "Solid, guard that date with your fuckin' life." And I did.

If it sounds intense, it kind of was, there was even a slight bro energy to all of it but remember, for most of these guys the alternative was prison or death, it was like we were all on our ninth life and we didn't want to blow it. We laughed hard and cried hard, like Marvin said.

The men in that room, me included, walked in there incomplete. We needed rearing, softening, finishing, we needed to grow up. What I inevitably learned there was no different from the age-old truths you might learn in a church, synagogue, mosque, a therapist's office, or a self-help book, it was just repackaged so that someone like me could understand it. Accountability, honor, gratitude, acceptance, restraint of pen and tongue, treating others the way you want to be treated, dignity, faith, all tenets we know have worked throughout history, but not all of us were taught.

Eventually, it became about more than not drinking and using. It became about growing into someone I was proud to be. Some people walk into meetings and their only interest is getting sober, that's it. They like themselves just fine and were it not for this pesky drinking habit, they would have it all figured out. I wasn't like that. Once you took away the drink, the drug, the girl, etc., I was forced to face myself. Did I like this person staring back at me? Obviously not. I mean, I had tried to kill him for so long.

All of this and I'd only been sober a year. The universe had sort of gifted me this time, because the first six months of it were spent doing publicity for *The Wackness*. I got to be sober and present while going around the country, promoting this thing I was truly proud of. I wasn't bogged down by professional fear because it seemed like things, at least for the moment, were going to work out. I went to meetings, I did press, and I went on my own little emotional tour, reintroducing myself to friends who had been so worried about me. It wasn't an amends process per se, that was different, this was just sort of showing my face again, around the people who had written me off as "the druggie." Even my mom, who had seen me through the process, said at dinner, a few months after I got sober, "I feel like I have my son back." Ooof, you'll never truly see the damage you've caused till the rain stops pouring and the wind dies down.

When I lost weight, there was no manual at the finish line, no plan for what was next. I thought once there was a particular number on the scale I would be freed of my past and ready to take on the world. Similarly when I got sober, I thought I had conquered my innermost demons and found a new way to live. All of that was true but only to a point. Losing weight allowed me admittance to the game, but now I had to hit a home run, and getting sober allowed me to see how much work there was to be done. I was no longer carpet bombing my life with bad behavior but now the city had to be rebuilt.

I was twenty-two and I didn't know that the next decade of my life would be the most challenging period of growth I'd ever faced. I didn't know that any preconceptions I had of where I thought my life was going would have to be shattered. I had been stilted, arrested, and numbed up, but now it was time to grow, in overdrive. The universe got me sober, it gave me the tools and support for what was about to come next, but this was some real hero's journey shit and I had no idea what I was in for.

My ego would have to be smashed, and I had the perfect job to do it.[1]

---

1   As I write this, I'm two weeks short of thirteen years sober, and hopefully by the time this book comes out, I still will be. I don't speak in absolutes because I've known too many people whose life got too good too quickly and suddenly a drink didn't sound that bad anymore. So in sticking with the whole one day at a time of it all, I cannot guarantee that I will die sober, but I can guarantee that I will go to sleep tonight without a drink. I'll tell you that today I still go to meetings regularly, I have a sponsor whom I speak to regularly, and a group of sober people who are my best friends. Everything good in my life is because of sobriety.

Writing this chapter was tricky because of the anonymous nature of the twelve-step program. I mulled over how I might talk about this part of my life in detail while still honoring the anonymity of the twelve steps. And while, to the best of my ability, I think I was able to share with you my particular experience and mine alone, there'll still be people who disagree with me mentioning AA at all.

So I'll give this disclaimer:

I am in no shape or form a representative, spokesman, or ambassador for Alcoholics Anonymous or any other twelve-step program. I, like millions of others, have benefited from recovery and the twelve steps, this is just my experience of getting sober, there are many ways to do it, but this one is mine. And if one day I am no longer sober, it will not be because AA failed me, it will be of my own volition.

The decision and any blame will lie with me, not AA or any other twelve-step program.

When I interviewed Steve-O, *Jackass* star and sober dude, for the *CURIOUS* podcast, he said "Ya know, no one ever accuses the gym of not working when people gain weight; they just assume that person stopped going."

11

The Fourth Hemsworth Brother

I'm running down the middle of the street in downtown Detroit, there're explosions going off on either side of me, I've got an AK-47 strapped to my shoulder, cameras mounted on cranes and helicopters filming me, and all I can think is *I'm fucking this up.*

I want to talk about the duality of ego for a minute. It would be absurd to think that I could have made it to this point. Do your best to not do the knee-jerk, but-Josh-you-had-so-much-going-for-you reaction here, I appreciate the pathos but let's actually look at this through the lens of logic. My birth was fraught with impossibility, my mom being a single mother and managing to support us was slightly if not completely remarkable. The fact that I was able to jump headfirst into a profession at a time when most kids are getting fitted for braces, with no connections, no in, no nepotism in sight, again, absurd. And to have made it all the way to this point one hundred pounds lighter, sober, and on the precipice of actually shedding the child star image? Insane.

I'm not trying to take a victory lap here, in fact we're a few paragraphs away from me completely burning down the whole enterprise AGAIN so strap in. What I'm trying to highlight is what is required to surmount this kind of task. In 1964, Muhammad Ali stood over Sonny Liston and screamed, "I AM THE GREATEST." Even more interesting though, is when Ali said, "I am the greatest, I said that even before I knew I was." I said that even before I knew I was, is what I'm getting at here. This idea that some version of self-hypnosis, self-deception, self-manifestation is required for anyone to become the best at anything. And sometimes not even the best but pretty good or even okay at it. Ali had to *believe* he was the greatest for the world to know it too.

I think you would be hard pressed to find anyone who didn't have to thoroughly brainwash themselves to deny the very prescient and real obstacles they could face. You could call it confidence, you could call it faith, you could even call it belief but, for me, I'm going to call it ego.

Ego is what got me through those impossible nights when I lost the battle again and again over whether to call the pizza guy for the umpteenth time. "You'll do it Josh, you'll lose the weight one day, I know you'll do it." "Yeah, yeah, yeah, where's the ranch?" Ego is what told me at twelve years old that I deserved to be on the biggest kids' show on television with basically no experience. Ego is what pushed me at twenty to turn my back on everything that had ever worked for me and try to make it as a real actor.

Ego, it's a funny thing. We need it, in moments of extreme adversity; that voice, that inner Joe Pesci, can sometimes be the only thing that pushes you to get out of bed in the morning. Fuck 'em, fuck 'em all, we'll prove 'em all wrong, we'll show them. And sometimes you do.

The funny thing about Joe Pesci, though, is that he starts off as your favorite character of every movie and then eventually and almost certainly gets the protagonist killed or close to it. Ego had delivered me to this moment, it had quelled the fear, the second guessing, and told me that I DESERVED to be here.

But once I was "here," once I had arrived, that unchecked ego continued to bark orders at me. It told me I was ready for something I wasn't, it told me I could fake it till I made it, it told me I was the best.

Ego is what delivered me, it's also what totally screwed me.

Six months earlier:

Agent: You've been offered to play Chris Hemsworth's brother in the remake of the movie *Red Dawn*. It's a big, sixty-million-dollar action movie for MGM, and you two would be the stars. The producers saw *The Wackness* and think you're the guy. What do you think?

Me: Who would believe Chris Hemsworth and I are brothers?

Okay, I didn't say that. I didn't say anything NEAR that. I said yes because this all made perfect sense. I was a year sober, I was fit, I no longer looked like the walking dead, and I was starting to resemble a respectable member of society. This was it, my shot, the thing I'd worked my entire life for, I had shown what I could do and now it was time for a major studio to mount a multimillion-dollar franchise on my shoulders.

Finally, God and I were on the same page.

They say in sobriety, the amount of time you have sober is a representation of your emotional maturity. So if you're fifteen years sober, you're basically a teenager. I was a year sober, which made me a toddler. Ya know what toddlers are good at? Nothing, they're not actually good at anything.

Nor should they be cast in Blockbuster movies.

First up? I'd have to get in proper shape for the movie, like any respectable action star, so the producers set me up with the trainers from the movie *300*. I'd seen Gerard Butler's abs, they were good, damn good, maybe some of the best, and now it was my time to be 2 percent body fat and 100 percent the fucking man. Ryan Reynolds, Hugh Jackman, they transformed. Josh Peck? You best BELIEVE I'll be transforming.

I pulled up to a warehouse in an industrial part of LA for my first day of training. Athleisure wear hugging my formidable thighs, I stepped out of my car a man on a mission. This was no Planet Fitness, my friends, this looked like an Amazon warehouse dedicated to GUY SHIT. There were swords hanging from the walls, people deadlifting six hundred pounds, I felt like I was inside the Rock's mind. I walked in and was greeted by two former US Navy SEALs, Logan and Dave. Navy SEALs. The most elite fighting force in the world and Josh from *Drake & Josh*. Same thing. "We'll take it easy today, get a baseline for where you're at physically and then go from there."

They put me through a workout that crippled me. When I say crippled, I mean it in the classic sense in that I no longer had access to my legs or arms. It was unlike anything I'd ever done considering my usual workouts were push-ups with towels wrapped around my waist. I was rowing thousands of meters, doing deadlifts, carrying heavy kettlebells, and running sprints, round after round. I wasn't sore, I was immobile.

I knew it wouldn't be easy but I wasn't going to let a couple of Epsom salt baths and protein shakes get in the way of my dream. This was my time. I showed up six days a week, sometimes hobbling from the workout the day before. Luckily for me, Logan and Dave were two of the most supportive killing machines I had ever met. I went from 190 to 175 pounds, put on muscle, and made huge improvements in my overall functional fitness, improvements that would serve me for the rest of my life.

"Yeah yeah, so how'd you mess it up, Josh?" Jeez, dear reader, where is this coming from? Okay, I'll tell you.

Unfortunately, weighing three hundred pounds will alter your body forever, I don't care who you are. Unless you're six-four and a nose guard for the New York Jets, there's a good chance that even if you lose weight, your body won't snap back perfectly. I HAD gotten in great shape with the help of Logan and Dave, I WAS the lowest I'd ever weighed without the help of Colombian diet meds (cocaine, I'm referring to cocaine), but it wasn't perfect. I had some skin in places I shouldn't, some stretch marks in places I wouldn't want you to see. I looked extremely human but this was not acceptable because action stars don't look human, even Paul Rudd, who plays a superhero named ANTMAN, is jacked.

It was in that moment, under the cover of fear and insecurity, that ego truly took over.

Ego hijacked my thinking and suddenly there was a drunk captain at the helm of the ship steering us straight for an iceberg. It didn't matter that the producers had eyes and probably knew when they hired me that I wasn't going to be the shirt-off guy. It. Didn't. Matter. I had this idealized, MAN-DONIS image of myself that I had dreamt of since I was twelve, and I was going to become it, whether you liked it or not. Shirt off or shirt on.

The moment I felt like I couldn't achieve physically what was required was when I began to throw away everything that had EVER worked for me. Instead of doing all the things that made the producers like me in the first place, all the things that made them hire me, I created a false persona, a projection of what I thought they wanted, of what I thought YOU wanted.

I abandoned any skill set I had and instead of feeling like an impostor, I became one. I was a guy in a motorcycle jacket with no motorcycle.

Let me give you a couple of fun snapshots of how things promptly and thoroughly went off the rails.

June

I decide to grow my hair out, a friend shows me a picture of young Tom Brady. And because I'm playing a high school quarterback in the film, naturally I thought I should have the same look. I have the coarse Jewish hair of a person who probably roamed the Middle East for the past two thousand years, so for me to grow it out, I had to chemically straighten my hair to where it became bone straight. I looked like a fifties housewife, I looked like the neighbor who hands out toothbrushes on Halloween, the only thing relaxed about me was my hair.

July

They have me do chemistry reads with a bunch of actresses auditioning to play my girlfriend in the movie. They cast an actress named Isabel Lucas and I promptly fall in love with her. Nothing ever happens between us because I'm so crippled by her beauty that I actually hide from her most days like she was the police and I had a warrant.

August

I fly to Michigan and production immediately enrolls me in football training camp with real college football players. I suck, I fucking suck, and everyone knows it. This only makes me spin deeper into my E Hole, that's ego hole for all of you new to a phrase I just came up with. I learn to throw a football with a tight spiral but everything else is straight trash, I know it, they know it, the players are sweet and supportive but only because they're being paid to be there. After two weeks, the director and all the producers come to watch my progress and the coaches who had been training us make a *very* big deal of this. Don't worry, Coach! I'll let ya down!

Typically, actually always, the quarterback (me) stands behind his center, in this case mine was a three-hundred-pound Black dude named Reggie, and gets snapped the ball when he yells "Hut!" Whelp, on the first play, as the entire creative team behind the movie watched, I walked up to take the snap and realized that Reggie had transformed into a two-hundred-pound white guy. That's right, I lined up behind the wrong guy. Jesus, maybe my dad was right to split.

September

We start shooting.

I'm a mess. From day one I am a mess and it doesn't let up for the next four months of shooting. Almost every day on the set I am overcome by a deep feeling of imminent disaster, like a pyromaniac sitting next to a lighter shop. I was going to be responsible for my own demise and THERE WAS NOTHING I COULD DO ABOUT IT.

"Hey Josh, when you say 'mess,' what do you mean?"

Whether it was training with the US Navy SEALs or football camp, I couldn't reconcile that I wasn't good at these things. My ego couldn't handle that I wasn't living up to this idealized image of myself. I wanted to be the man so bad, I'd been the sweet, butt-of-the-joke comedy guy my entire life and I just wanted to retire that image forever.

Plus, I was working opposite Chris Hemsworth, which was a whole other issue. Chris is a true alpha, an actual leader and I marveled as he easily committed to scenes that called on him to save the world. I trained with the guys who probably killed Bin Laden and I still would pick Chris to rescue me over them because he's THAT believable. Plus he was nice too?! Chris is short for Christ isn't it? Makes sense.

After a few weeks of filming, I realized my problem, I just needed to be more like Chris.

Here's where things got really weird. I developed a persona of what I thought the Josh version of Chris would be. I lowered my voice—I'm laughing as I write this—I stood differently, and the worst part is, I mugged. I strained my face into this contorted half Clint Eastwood, half Robert Pattinson in *Twilight* type face to exude the level of cool I thought was required.

It did not translate.

I was melodramatic, eating up the scenery in every scene to show the world, and especially Isabel Lucas, what an incredible actor I was. I would make myself cry unnecessarily just because I could. If the scene called for anger, I would blow my top like someone cut me off in traffic, and worst of all, in many of the scenes, I did nothing. I just stood there trying to look cool and tortured like I was a Parisian model with a personality disorder.

Lee Strasberg once said, "Fear and tension interrupts expression." Whelp, that was the only way to describe my performance, tense. I was trying to be like, like Chris, like Logan and Dave, when the only person they needed me to be was Josh Peck.

Unfortunately, Josh had left the building.

I wish someone had said something. I wish the director or one of the producers had pulled me aside and said "What the hell are you doing, are you having a stroke? Do you need medical assistance?" I wish they would have shown me footage while we were shooting, so I could've seen how ridiculous I was, how overwrought, and fixed it. But maybe it was too late. Maybe they were too deep into filming by the time they realized it, and by then to fire me would've cost too much money to reshoot it.

I don't know, and I appreciate them for not firing me, I think. To be honest, I'm not sure even if the director *had* taken me aside and said, "Hey, do a little less" or "Just be yourself," I would've been able to really hear it. Because I didn't know who myself was. I knew I didn't want to be the old Josh, that I knew for sure and I could have sworn I wanted to be this guy, this badass, football-playing, pretty-girl-dating, world-saving hero, but I sucked at it. I was just doing a bad impression.

I was sober physically but not mentally. I was trying to bend the world to my will, forcing people to see me the way I thought they should. Instead of being of service to the producers, to the script, to my fellow actors, I was in service only to myself and it showed. I was, yet again, the same head in a new body. It wasn't the same as when I was using, but it put me in a similar position, out of control and unreliable. This wasn't what sobriety had taught me and it surely wasn't what those guys in my men's meetings were talking about each week.

I heard a guy once say "If you're a bank robber and you get sober, it'll just make you a better bank robber. Putting down the bottle, that's the first step, but what comes next is the real work, the emotional sobriety that's required to actually have a good life." It was never more clear than in this moment how much work I still had to do.

The moment we finished the movie, I knew it was bad, I didn't know how bad but it's like a test you don't finish in time, there's no chance you got an A, it's just whether or not you got a D or an F. For the year that followed, when people would ask me what I was working on, I'd watch as their eyes lit up, all they heard was a big action movie. I didn't have the heart to tell them I had spent four months successfully sabotaging myself.

Six months had passed and they invited some of the cast to watch a rough cut of the movie at a screening room in Century City. I showed up, found a seat next to my cast-mates, and right at that moment thought, *Maybe it's not that bad, in fact, maybe it'll be good.* I had shared my fears with so many people by now that I was starting to believe them when they would say "Everyone is their own worst critic!" and "Editing does wonders." Maybe I was crazy.

So, good news, I'm not crazy. I was, in fact, shit. I mean look, it's not a student film, obviously it wasn't a complete Dumpster fire, but it was pretty damn close, and eventually the reviews of my performance specifically would agree. Here it is, the movie was fine—I was bad. I remember going out for dinner after the screening with my friend Julian, who was also in the movie. We went to the Woodfire Ranch Grill, which everyone knows is a happy place, and I proceeded to gorge myself on as many carbs as I could. I was looking for anything remotely acceptable for me to completely drown my sorrows in, I wasn't going to drink, but I wanted to. The restaurant wasn't far from my mom's, and I showed up at her house at about 11:00 p.m., sat on her bed, stared out the window, and cried. Pitiful.

Oh, and here's the best part. The moment we finished the film, MGM went bankrupt. That's right, the film studio that had made the movie no longer had the money to distribute it. So instead of it coming out a year later, like most movies, it got held for three years. It was like a three-year pregnancy knowing you're going to give birth to a kid you'll hate.

I think back on this time in my life, shooting the film and after, and how much it affected me. I remember telling people, my life either existed BRD or ARD. Before *Red Dawn* or After *Red Dawn*. It wasn't about the movie, forget the movie. It's what that experience did to me, or more specifically what I let it do to me. It validated my worst fear, that I was never meant for this. That no matter how hard I tried, no matter how much I changed my appearance, I just didn't have what it took. I started getting bad feedback in auditions because they could smell me as I walked in the room, it was like the stench of someone who just got dumped, no one wants to date that guy.

So there I was living in these two worlds, I was twenty-three, staying sober, doing the right thing, and surviving while simultaneously being terrified about what was going to happen next. I knew a glitch had occurred, I was off track as an actor, but I didn't know how to fix it. Acting had been the only thing in life I thought I was any good at until that point, so if that was no longer true, what was I going to do?

It was going to be a rough ten years.

12

Premium Economy
to Bali

Someone I've never met, in a country I've never been to, has just wired me $5,000. It's a test because a few weeks later, they'd send me another $50K. I didn't know that accepting this money meant entering into a life I'd never expected.

Let's pick up where we left off. It's 2013, I'm twenty-six, *Red Dawn* finally comes out in November 2012—three years after we finished filming and the world didn't end when people saw my performance. Let's be clear, they weren't happy with it, I got the shit kicked out of me in the reviews, but still, to my surprise—it came and went. I'd spent three years crippled by the idea of people seeing it—I prayed every night that it wouldn't come out, but when it finally did come out, it was almost a relief. I had stood on the executioner's block and realized I could live through a couple of bad reviews or even a lot of them.

Thankfully, throughout this process, I was sober but

now I had the added benefit of being in pain, which is always a good motivator. I never stopped attending meetings, but now I was ready to level up and confront the thing that got me here. I had to or risk drinking again, it just hurt too much. I'd stare Joe Pesci in the face and say, "Thanks for getting us this far, but I think it's time we parted ways." I knew I'd never completely eradicate myself from ego, from fear, from insecurity, but I'd get better at not reacting to it. Live in the world that is, instead of the world you think you deserve, someone once told me. Every meeting I went to, I'd listen to people struggling to get sober, people who couldn't even put a day together, and I was reminded of how lucky I was, how good I had it.

I had no momentum, though, no "heat," which is a Hollywood term for lack of temperature. I was dead in the water, back of the line. I had been given a chance and failed, so I'd have to sit in a waiting room with fifty other guys who looked like me again, waiting to audition for the part of the know-it-all computer nerd on whatever new cop drama was casting. I was both hurt and relieved, I mean my ego couldn't stand it—there I was facing off against Joe Blow, who moved here from Mount St. wherever the fuck to try acting, and all I wanted to say was "I was so close to never having to do this again!"

Most actors hate auditioning, and who can blame them? There are few professions other than sales and real estate where you're constantly interviewing for your next job. And even if you do land a big job, how long does that last? Three months? Six if there's a superhero involved. The whole goal of any actor is to become successful enough to not have to audition anymore.

But I've spent my entire life auditioning—I'd been doing it since I was ten, from sitting in cattle calls of a hundred tweens to sitting in front of fifteen network execs at a screen test (when it's down to two or three people for a role and you have to audition in front of the entire network). Spend enough time in the shit, and eventually it just starts to feel like home, I guess. It was fun to get a sneak peek at the good life, to breathe the rarefied air of the supersuccessful, but this was home.

Between ages twenty-three and twenty-six, I would act in three films. A thriller called *ATM*, where I'm stuck in an ATM vestibule being stalked by a killer—Rotten Tomatoes score 16; a 3-D dance movie starring Chris Brown—Rotten Tomatoes score 8; and a cold weather Western that shot in minus-forty-degree weather . . . in Romania—Rotten Tomatoes score 0 because it never officially came out. Not great movies, but I was grateful to have the work, I knew these films weren't going to change my life, but I wasn't in that mind-set, I was just happy to pay my rent.

These movies each paid something called Schedule F, which is a Screen Actors Guild contractual term for $80k. After 20 percent to agents and manager and 30 percent to

Uncle Sam, I was clearing $40k. So I was making a living as an actor, on the salary of a waiter and spending the rest of my time working at my other passion, existential dread. I wasn't wrong to be worried, I knew I was dipping my toe in precarious waters, you have to be careful when taking jobs just to survive in show business, because people can tell. Also, once those jobs run out, what do you do?

I had to do something. When I got sober the idea had been ingrained in me that doing the same thing and expecting a different result was the definition of insanity. I knew something had to change, but what? All I had ever done was throw myself at the altar of show business and prayed someone picked me. You might be thinking, *You were twenty-six, Josh, come on, who has their entire life figured out at that age?* You're not wrong except that I had a mom who was almost seventy at that point and whom I had been taking care of since I was sixteen. I knew I'd be okay—I could sleep on a friend's couch if I had to—but who would take care of her? She had given up her life in New York for me, relocated at almost sixty to support my career. It was my turn to support her and I'd rather die than put her out.

I'd devoted my entire life to this thing, no college, no backup plan, and nothing on the horizon. I was scared, I had considered getting out, maybe finding a traditional job, but what? I had no other skills for anything.

Or so I thought.

In the early 2000s, a confluence of events occurred that would benefit me a decade later. It would allow me to create a new career for myself that would become more fruitful than acting ever was, and it all started at this little school in Cambridge.

In 2003 an underachieving Harvard dropout named Mark Zuckerberg started a website called Facebook, which subsequently became the mother of all social media. Others had existed before it, such as MySpace and Friendster. But none made quite the impact Facebook did. A few years later, Google bought a little video-sharing website called YouTube. After that three guys named Evan Williams, Biz Stone, and Jack Dorsey started a company called Twitter. And finally, in 2012, Facebook bought a photo-sharing app called Instagram and so spawned the age of social media. Snapchat's in there too.

In 2012, on the app store, a new video-sharing app appeared called Vine. It was much like Instagram, except instead of pictures it was video, six-second videos, in fact—that was the time limit. Within three months of launching, it was acquired by Twitter, and by April 13, 2013, it was the number one downloaded app on the iOS app store. Twitter had been around for a while, Ashton Kutcher used it, Instagram was less popular but growing, and then there was Vine. If Twitter was for Ashton and Instagram was for the attractive, then Vine was for funny people who didn't have a steady paycheck.

And I was a fan.

My girlfriend Paige, who would later become my wife, and I would sit around watching videos, sharing them over text and turning people onto the app. I mean how rarely do you get to be part of the start of something? Most people don't even know what you are talking about? It was March, so the app had only been out a few months, but as soon as they watched, they were hooked. Vine was growing fast, really fast—it seemed like everyone was discovering it.

"You should make one," Paige said one afternoon as we cackled, watching. Until that point I had been pretty resistant to social media; in fact it seemed I was resistant to any success considering every decision I made led me deeper into unemployment. I was trying and failing at being a "real actor," which I thought meant being mysterious, edgy, aloof, and inaccessible. But social media seemed like the height of accessibility. I very badly wanted to detach from the old image people had of me and in doing so help them forget I ever existed.

So there I was, yet again beaten into a state of willingness, my way had gotten me here, and I figured, why not? What did I have to lose? I couldn't become more unemployed. What happened next was an alchemy of timing, luck, and some talent, which, as far as I can tell, is the recipe for all success.

Guided by Paige, I made my first Vine. The whole

thing took me five minutes. It was fine, not bad, kind of funny, fine. I don't even remember it, which says something. I think I was making fun of the fact that my car had to be towed because of a flat tire. I made a few more Vines over the next week that were slightly better, funnier, but still just fine. I was a recreational user like everyone else, just doing it for fun.

Until the next week, when I was sitting at lunch having just uploaded my fourth video and got a text from a friend that read, "Okay popular page." "What?" I replied. "You're on the Vine popular page." Now, I didn't even know Vine had a popular page. But there I was, showcased with a few other creators whose videos were also doing well that day. Of all the videos on the app, at that moment mine was the most popular.

Weird.

How'd that happen?

Here's my guess.

Vine had been purchased by Twitter in 2012, so there was a synchronization between the two apps, allowing Vines to be broadcast to your Twitter followers. I had joined Twitter in 2009 and abandoned it shortly after, but I had small following of fifteen thousand followers, not a lot but enough. So when I uploaded my first Vines, people saw them, enough to trigger the algorithm to deliver it to more people.

Then there was the timing, the app was new, there

simply weren't that many creators on it. There were plenty of people watching Vines but not many people making them, so if there was anything even remotely entertaining, you were going to get eyes on it. It wasn't the orgy of content that's available today.

And finally, I guess the intangible part, I had weirdly been preparing for this moment my entire life. It sounds ridiculous, I know, I feel funny saying it, but it's true. The genius of Vine was the format, six seconds. You had six seconds to tell your joke, to make people feel something, that's it. It turned out this proved quite hard for most people, because most Vines were a Dumpster fire. Everyone could take a cool photo for IG and there were plenty of smart people tweeting, but making a good video in six seconds? Trickier.

There's a Mark Twain quote that says "If I had more time, I would have written a shorter letter." Comedy is economy. How can you do the most with the least? No one's ever said about a joke "It's not wordy enough." As far as Vine went, it was simple, get out a setup and a punch line before the timer runs out. I had been doing that my whole life, since watching TV when I was eight, the music was in my head. The thing that was a downfall with acting—my big, shticky, sitcom sense of humor—was suddenly perfect for this.

I started showing up on the popular page every time I posted a video, which in turn aggregated more people to my page. I was growing fast, really fast—almost 100k followers a day. People started taking notice, and by June I was getting recognized for my Vine videos more than anything else. Hundreds of thousands of people were downloading the app every day, and when they opened it, there was a good chance my stupid face would greet them.

There was something in the air, something was changing—it was weird to be getting recognition for this thing I honestly wasn't taking super seriously. I mean what were these videos I was making? They were my greatest hits, funny stories or characters I'd done around my friends forever, random musings I'd perform as I sat in traffic (don't text and drive), silly songs I'd write at the piano when I was bored. I was used to things taking eighteen months to come out, that required hundreds of people and millions of dollars to execute, and here I was, coming up with an idea, shooting and delivering it within minutes. It was just so different.

At about this time, I got a phone call from my agent and manager. I don't know how they were alerted to my new hobby but they were . . . curious. "Um, what is this? You're making wacky videos in your car? Our goal has been to get you serious roles, to make you a leading man. Do you think this hurts us?" I knew what a phone call like this meant. They weren't wrong in bringing it up, I mean, does this hurt me? I don't know. I'm sure they were wondering what, if anything, was next for me and they certainly weren't expecting this new side hustle. If there was a time to drop me as their client it was now, but luckily, none of us could pass judgment on this thing because no one knew what it was yet. Not me, not them, no one.

I was operating in the dark, I had no frame of reference. I enjoyed making these videos because it felt good to be creative every day and there were no stakes, it was just fun and what was even more fun was having people repeat the videos to me at supermarkets. I was quotable! But eventually as more people started to notice, I thought I should really give this some thought, it felt like this was an inflection point, I could quit now and get out clean, or really lean in and see what happened.

I sought my friend Rami's counsel. Rami had recently helped found a company called The Audience, which pioneered influencer marketing. Their mission was simple, get Fortune 500 companies to take a little bit of their billion-dollar marketing budget and convince them to spend it on Facebook, Instagram, Snapchat, and Twitter instead of traditional media such as commercials, print ads, and radio. I needed help and Rami, being a good friend and someone whose insight I really trusted, was the first person I went to. He gave me what would turn out to be perfect, almost proleptic advice.

"No one knows what this is, Josh. Don't let your agents, your friends, anyone tell you because even I don't know, it's too early. But I'll tell you this, being able to affect your audience, to reach hundreds of thousands of people, to connect with them, hear what they like, what they don't like and to be able to share with them something you've created? That's powerful. So keep doing it. In fact, do it every day."

It sounds simple, right? Especially now, when all of this is part of our daily lives, but back then there were no examples, no case studies, no rules. There wasn't the Rock Instagramming his cheat meals to two hundred million people or the president using Twitter to debate climate change.

I listened to Rami, because he's an Apostle. I leaned in. If I could've snapped my fingers and become Leonardo DiCaprio in that moment I would've but I couldn't. What I could do is make more videos. I made one every day, and it turns out the algorithm shines brightly on those who feed it because by August I was the number one person on Vine, overtaking Harry Styles with 3.5 million followers. And while Harry will always be an icon and have a lower BMI than me, I hope to one day bring this up to him as I gaze at his perfect bone structure whilst his security has me removed.

I wouldn't stay number one for long but I would remain one of the top creators and the by-product was that my Instagram and Twitter grew, creating this ecosystem of different places I could create. Communications theorist Marshall McLuhan said, "The medium is the message."

Suddenly I had multiple mediums at my disposal. If I had a thought, a static image, or a funny video that I thought was interesting, I had somewhere to display it and an audience who was hungry for it.

This is all cute, Josh, but what about the money?

Industrious friends of mine started bringing up monetizing my following because (a) people love money and (b) when you're commanding a big audience, monetization is the natural next step. Brands don't pay a 10x multiple to run a commercial during the Super Bowl for the love of the game, they do it because it has the most eyeballs. Vine was certainly going to make money off the content we were creating, and maybe that could apply to the creators too?

At least that was the thought. By then the only rumors of people making money from social media were for Kim Kardashian getting paid to tweet out her favorite FitTea. Honestly, I was just happy to have somewhere to create, somewhere to stay relevant until I got my next gig. In fact, my big hope from all this was if it came down to me and another actor for a role, some forward-thinking executive would look at both our social presence and say, "Give it to the guy with more followers, he can help publicize the movie." If the scales were even and both actors were qualified for the job, I'd happily take the advantage. I needed it.

Slowly but surely, though, major brands did start to advertise on the app. Content creators with similar followings started incorporating McDonald's or Boost Mobile into their videos and I assumed they weren't doing it for gift cards and free wireless plans. So I created an email account and displayed it on my profile, hoping that if the opportunity was there, they would know where to find me.

BUSINESS: *JOSHPECKVINE@GMAIL.COM*

Simple, to the point. I mean business and if *you* mean business, email this random Gmail account that doesn't even remotely look official. I started getting emails right away, mostly from fans of *Drake & Josh*, asking if they could have my phone number or telling me I sucked, maybe this wasn't the gold mine I was hoping for. And then one day, in June of 2014, an email came in that would change everything.

> Hi Josh!
>
> We are big fans of you here at BADOO, the hottest new dating app, and we would love to do Vine with you to help promote our app. Would five thousand dollars be agreeable? We would like the promotion to go live by the end of the week.
>
> Thanks and hope to hear from you!

Now, McDonald's and Boost Mobile are one thing, but an email from an app I've never heard of? THAT seemed promising. In reality, I had seen plenty of people advertising BADOO already. The company was based in Europe, had an unlimited supply of money, and let's just say a wide berth when it came to brand strategy. I have to give them credit though for recognizing social media marketing before many Fortune 500 companies.

I never met the person on the other side of that email, but I was ready to roll the dice. Why not? I wrote them back, presenting myself as Josh Peck's "social media manager" and agreed to the five thousand dollars and a date for the post. I made the video, sent it over for approval, and on the day it was set to go live thought, *Whelp, here goes nothing, if this all proves to be a farce, I'll take the video down.* But within minutes of posting the video, I got an alert from PayPal: five thousand dollars has been received from BADOO.

I couldn't believe it, it didn't seem real. I didn't even have a PayPal account until I created one for this campaign and suddenly I had $5k sitting in it? What seemed even more unreal was BADOO reaching out again with the same offer the following week: five thousand dollars for one video. I made four that month: $20k.

I had never, I repeat NEVER, been able to create an income stream outside of show business before. Every cent I made had to be approved by a team of casting directors, producers, studio executives, business affairs lawyers, and directors before it ever made its way to my pocket. But this was like sales: sell a car, get a commission. You were rewarded for your hard work, and it felt instant. If you worked hard enough, you got the check. It was so . . . logical? Now, $20k wasn't a huge amount of money, but if I could make that much every month, that was a living.

To make twenty thousand dollars a month meant simply that I wasn't on a tightrope for once in my life, or at least for the next few months. Sure, sailing out into rough seas is what makes a great sailor, but it never hurts to have one extra port. If this worked, I mean really worked, like I created an entirely new business for myself, it would be possible that my life and entire self-worth wouldn't have to be solely contingent on whether I became the next Shia LaBeouf. Trust me, it would still be majorly wrapped up in it, but at least I'd know I could survive and even, dare I say, live a little?

I'd met so many actors over the years who were now in their forties without a wife or kids because they just never had the security they needed to do it. They were always waiting for that next job, that next opportunity, that next what if. Living in a perpetual state of what if requires your life to be in some version of a holding pattern, it's just hard to progress. How do you take on the responsibility of a family, knowing this thing you've put your entire life into might not work out, that following your dream could bring your whole family down with you.

Nope, this was my chance, I called my girlfriend and said, "Do you want to go on vacation?" I'd never been on vacation before . . . strike that, I'd been to the Jersey Shore aka the Cancún of the Garden State, and overnight trips to San Diego, but I was twenty-seven and had yet to go on a proper vacation—one that required a plane and a passport. Even my dirtbag friends growing up would figure out a way to make it to the Bahamas once a year and I wanted to know what that felt like.

Paige had mentioned that friends were planning a trip to Bali at the end of the month and invited us to join them. Under normal circumstances I never would've agreed, it would've felt extravagant and too long to be away, I always had to focus on getting a gig. What if I get an audition while we're away? What if I'm still not working in a few months and I could've used that money for rent? You see?

What if, what if, what if.

But this was different. Without thinking twice I told her to book the trip, which was new for me, I think twice about everything at a minimum and three or four times just for good measure. But on some level I knew if I could make this money now and my following was only increasing, what could I make the next month? Or the month after? By now I had been doing this for a year and it didn't seem like social media was going anywhere, it was getting stronger.

I deviated. For the second time in my life I realized my way wasn't working, and tried it someone else's way. The first time, it got me sober, I listened to Marvin, my mom, and the other people in the rooms of Alcoholics Anonymous and my life improved dramatically.

This second time, I listened to Paige, I listened to Rami. and I listened to the comments section, telling me every day what they liked and didn't like about what I was posting.

I had tried for so long to be the master of my own destiny, to be at the controls of my life, and my career, and I had proven to be a deeply imperfect captain. But now, this time, I was doing it someone else's way, letting the wind take me where it would. My life went into overdrive and I couldn't wait.

13

Fortune Five
Hundy Money

Miami 2014

Steve Aoki, world-renowned DJ, entrepreneur, and son of
Rocky Aoki, owner and creator of Benihana, no big deal,
is performing at LIV nightclub in Miami. Fifteen hundred
bodies press tightly together as eurotrash millionaires buy
bottles of overpriced liquor for their overpriced compan-
ions. I'm standing behind Steve, watching as he controls
the audience like a conductor, with every button he hits,
every knob he turns, the audience reacts on cue, twisting,
jumping, and grinding together. Steve turns back, sees me
standing behind him, and whispers,

"Want to get onstage with me?"

Of course I want to get onstage with you, Steve Aoki.

Twenty-Four Hours Earlier

I'm boarding a flight to Florida. My friend Rami, an authority on all things social media, has been given the task

of convincing the president of iHeartRadio to give up a portion of his marketing budget for the year. In 2014, iHeart reached nine of every ten Americans through their radio stations and live events; if they could be swayed to invest even a small amount of money in a new thing called "influencer marketing" it would be a huge get.

Think about advertising trends over the past few centuries. With the advent of the printing press in 1450, print advertising reigned supreme for hundreds of years, only to be usurped by radio, then television, and forty years later the internet. That's four mediums over five hundred years. Was social media going to be the fifth? Probably, but no one knew that for sure, especially the people with all the money. Everyone can spot a good idea once it's been proven, but did you have the guts to invest when it mattered?

Rami had a plan. He enlisted me and a few other "influencers" to show the power of social media. His idea was simple, let's bring the product to them. It was like a mobile trade show, don't believe our product works? Let me pour red wine on this carpet and show you how quickly the stain comes out with our new formula. Don't believe in influencer marketing? Let me show you how quickly a video Josh posts from your event is seen by hundreds of thousands of people.

Refresh, ten thousand views, refresh, fifty thousand views, refresh, a hundred thousand views, the evidence was irrefutable.

Now, I didn't expect to be sitting at a sushi restaurant

in South Beach explaining Vine to middle-aged executives, but I also didn't mind it. I'd never been to Miami before and I lived in South Florida as a kid, plus being there sure broke up the mundanity of waiting for my next audition and by that I mean my next rejection. This wasn't charity, I was getting paid to be there, to post on social media, to eat sushi with CEOs, and at the end of the night, to party onstage with Steve Aoki, who also wanted to know what this thing "Vine" was.

It wasn't my dream, but it didn't suck.

May 2015

I'm with a Chinese billionaire at the kind of restaurant in Beverly Hills reserved for Chinese billionaires. I've been asked to take over social media brand strategy for his budding energy drink company and I'm intrigued because unlike most energy drinks, it doesn't taste like transmission fluid. He offers me equity in the company instead of an upfront payment, and at this point I've learned that billionaires, while generous when it comes to Japanese steaks, are surprisingly cheap when it comes to actually paying you. Plus I didn't think there was a world in which I was going to fly to Hong Kong, ask him to open up his books if he didn't pay me, and return with all my extremities, so I politely decline. Before I leave, though, he offers me a ride in his Rolls-Royce to get a milk shake in West

Hollywood. I agree because while I'd had plenty of milk shakes, I'd never ridden in a Rolls-Royce.

The Rolls and the milk shake were both excellent.

September 2017

I'm sitting in a conference room at Wendy's headquarters in Columbus, Ohio. That's right, square burgers, dip-your-fries-in-your-softie Wendy's. Dave Thomas, redhead-on-the-logo Wendy's. I've been asked by the brand partnership division of Twitter, a division by this point I had done almost a million dollars in business with, to teach the Wendy's marketing team how to make viral social media content. A year later, I'd sit onstage with Wendy's CMO and some of the heads of Twitter, giving a presentation on brand strategy at Adweek in New York.

February 2019

It's the kind of cold day that people from the Midwest shrug off but if you're from anywhere else, hits you like a truck. I'm in Bloomington at Indiana University about to go in front of two thousand students who for some reason want to hear me speak. Me. A guy who's never been to college and didn't exactly graduate from high school. That's right parents, this is where your tuition's going. Half of the show will be stand-up, the other half will be a moderated

Q and A where I'll talk about my life, my career, and how I turned silly Vine videos into a thriving social media business. I'll wind up doing twelve talks like this that year.

March 2020

I've just gotten off a production call and I'm preparing to head to the NCAA Final Four in Atlanta for the fourth time with Buick. As one of the presenting sponsors of the weekend, I'll help lead Buick's social media initiative like I did when I first started working with them in 2017. We'll create content for the event, showcasing their new cars while tying it in with March Madness, but the best part will be getting to sit in some very respectable seats and watch the actual game. A week later the whole world will shut down and we'll put a rain check on the Final Four and basically life that year.

But Josh, I thought you were an actor. Me too.

Remember when Rami told me to lean in? To keep doing this? Well, after I made that money with BADOO, I was like a man on fire. It was 2014 and the experiment had worked, it turns out this hobby of mine, this tool I was using to hopefully get another acting job, any acting job, was actually proving to be quite lucrative. I was now cost positive, which is where any start-up wants to be, we're all on a "road to profitability," and this was all the data I needed. It was time to lean into this as fast and as hard as I could.

I had always lived in this slow progression, my life,

my career, an amalgamation of thousands of microtrans-actions that eventually, after decades, I hoped would culminate in some form of success. This wasn't like that, though, it felt immediate, like a glitch in the system, like I'd found a rigged slot machine and I needed to pull the lever as much as I could before they booted me out of the casino. In reality it was far from that, it was timing. I was one of the lucky few who was uniquely suited to exploit what was a renaissance in advertising.

Look, if you were a jujitsu master in the mid-1980s, your greatest hope was to open up a school or maybe a few of them and live off the money you made in tuition. Now, if you can incorporate some kickboxing, you can become the biggest star in the world fighting in the UFC. Even if you don't want to face off in the Octagon, the potential to create a franchise of schools or MMA-inspired gyms is so much greater because of the popularity of the sport. Similarly, if you were incredible at video games in the nineties, maybe you could compete for money or go work at a GameStop, but now thousands of people stream themselves playing video games every day, many of them making a living doing it and some a fortune.

This is what happened for me, I was in at the ground floor of what was becoming the greatest advertising revolution since television. No brand wanted to be last to the party, and the risk to reward was totally in their favor. They were used to handing tens of millions of dollars to advertising agencies for a couple of commercials, or they could roll the dice and hand over five hundred thousand to a budding brand agency, have it distributed among twenty people like me, and watch as the audience reach was comparable to that of any print or commercial ad they'd ever run.

It didn't have the cachet of traditional advertising yet, it lacked the prestige of some million-dollar ad campaign shot by Annie Leibovitz, but the eyes on it were undeniable. If you wanted people to see your product, putting it on the page of someone with a couple million followers would do it and there were analytics to prove it. Sure, you know how many people read the *New York Times*, but you have no idea whether they saw your ad on C2. With this, you knew how many people saw it, for how long, and whether or not they tapped the link to buy it.

We were also at a time when people were resisting curation. For so long print advertising looked like art and commercials were minimovies—sure we still bought stuff but I'm not sure anyone actually believed Matthew McConaughey drove a Lincoln. Social media advertising in its inherent low-fi felt like your friend was giving you a tip on a product they had just discovered. "Wow, Kim Kardashian really loves this FitTea and she's talking about it from her kitchen table, I guess I'll give it a try." We see it more than ever in podcasting, when Joe Rogan does an ad read, it's so much more impactful than some pre-recorded baritone using an announcer's voice.

When I got home from Bali, I combed the pages of Vine, Instagram, etc., to find all the different companies representing brands looking to get into what had been dubbed "influencer marketing." Companies with names such as Instafluence, Niche, Reach, and Gary Vaynerchuk's GrapeStory. I'd make an introduction through email or by phone, and soon I'd be on their roster, waiting to be called for their next campaign. There was no exclusivity, there still isn't. If you had enough followers, you qualified, and they were happy to have you because the wider array of influencers they had, the easier it was for them to satisfy whatever a brand was looking for. Everyone could eat.

The strategy was simple. Niche, for example, would retain the business of a massive company such as Wendy's or Bank of America, and promise them a certain amount of reach and impressions through their roster of influencers. It was no different than an ad agency guaranteeing five million views on a commercial, except they weren't buying time on a network, they were buying time on someone's Vine, YouTube, Instagram, or Facebook page. They were paying people like me to gain access to my millions of followers and you could be precise because whatever you were selling, there was an influencer for it. Gone were the days of putting up a billboard and hoping the right people saw it. If you wanted females between eighteen and twenty-five who were athletic to see your new gym shoe, there was someone with that exact audience.

At about this time, I also started reaching out to other creators. I'd sort of been out on my own island, creating videos by myself or with friends, but I knew there was a synergistic effect to collaborating with other people on the app. If you popped up on their page and they popped up on yours, you'd get exposure to a whole new audience. More followers meant bigger deals and I would see other people on Vine with big followings collaborating all the time; in fact, it seemed they had all moved from their respective hometowns to this one building in Hollywood, with the address—you guessed it—1600 Vine. Yup, I'm not kidding.

So here were these creators, these kids basically who were quickly becoming household names, making their own content for millions of people.

And then there was me, the guy from *Drake & Josh*.

I was sort of an outlier, I mean a lot of the people who become massively successful on social media come from relative obscurity, it's what makes it so compelling, right? Subverting the usual channels to attain success and cultivating an audience on their own? So many of the biggest names in social media today, be it Logan Paul or Mr. Beast, were high school students in small towns previous to this.

And then there was me, the guy from *Drake & Josh*.

It was odd for someone in my position to throw themselves so completely into social media the way I did. People used social media to go mainstream, not the other way around.

So when I asked these twentysomething creators if they wanted to shoot together sometime it was met with confusion. Trust me, I was confused too. I knew what the optics were—if you had some success as an actor, to take social media this seriously could be considered desperate. There was a clear distinction still, a ruling class, but less than five years later, that contrast between worlds would become almost invisible.

I didn't care, I was running with blinders on. I could wait and hope that the right job came around. Or I could do, for the first time, what felt good. Being productive felt good, and honestly, making money felt good. I'm not so sure it was driven by greed, I mean we did fly economy plus to Bali—I don't mean to brag, but it was the satisfaction you get from working hard and being compensated for it.

The time between paychecks as an actor can be so long that eventually when you do get paid, it can feel more like luck.

I've always sought security because my childhood was so chaotic, but this time, it was working to my advantage. Sometimes you have to go where it's warm.

Eventually I became friends with those top creators at 1600 Vine, we'd get together almost daily to work, to collaborate and to grow. They were my peers, we'd learn from each other, they were at the forefront of social media and understood it better than anyone else—they'd teach me how to edit, how to optimize videos, and how to groom an idea to be best suited for the platform it was on. "That has a sharper joke, put it on Vine. That premise sounds more family friendly, throw it on Facebook, there are so many moms on Facebook." I was happy to learn and happy to contribute a little bit of what I'd picked up over the years.

We were like a traveling theater company, a band of weirdos or, maybe more accurately, our own sketch comedy troupe. Every day we'd go through this truncated process of writing and producing our own stuff, someone would pitch an idea, we'd all weigh in with different thoughts, alternate jokes, and then we'd shoot it. Whoever idea it was would upload it to their page and boom, on to the next person. We'd rotate in and out of each other's Vines depending on what it called for but we constantly made ourselves available because everyone had the same goal, create more content.

It was like Andy Warhol's factory, just less sexy. I realize this wasn't exactly high art, I mean anyone who was a fan of Vine will tell you that. These were six-second comedy videos and sometimes it was easier to go with something relatable, such as "When your girlfriend won't give you the password to her cellphone," as a premise than to really dig for something great. But regardless of whether you were serving a five-course meal or fast food, there was an audience for it. The people on the apps wanted to be fed, they preferred it to be great, but they'd take something that was good or even okay as long as we kept giving it. Consistency was key and we knew that, so for the dozen of us top creators on Vine, this routine of making videos every day was just that, routine.

Eventually, the advertisers came, and they never stopped.

A month after my first deal, I got my next offer from a little company called Ford. That's right, F-150, built Ford tough, Ford. This was fortune five hundy money. They wanted two Vines and an Instagram post for sixteen thousand dollars. I'd have to produce the ads myself but I was already making Vines every day. Now I just had to figure out how to incorporate a car into it? Not a problem.

This was August 2014, and by the end of the year I'd worked with Mountain Dew, Anheuser-Busch, Hewlett Packard, Microsoft, and McDonald's. I'd make more in four months than I had the past three years combined and the work kept coming.

In the first four months of 2015, I doubled what I made the year before. I started to contemplate things I'd never thought about, maybe I'd propose to my girlfriend, maybe I'd buy a house. I wasn't rushing into it, I knew better than to make the rookie mistake of acting like the money you're making today is the money you'll make forever. But it was exciting, my life was upgrading because it wasn't solely based on things out of my control. The more content I made, the better it did, the more opportunities there were.

Being a kid actor had uniquely equipped me for what was required for this new business. I was conditioned to know my lines, stand on my mark, and deliver them on time, over and over again until it was perfect. That same self-discipline was required when you were on a deadline to shoot and deliver content for a Fortune 500 company, take their notes, and communicate in a way that satisfied the brand without feeling like a complete sellout.

The best part though, truly, was the ability to be creative every day. I've always been jealous of the musician who can practice a guitar riff till their fingers bleed or the writer who can sharpen their skills in front of a blank page completely on their own. They can do their art in a fully realized way without anyone's permission. Acting, though, is tougher. You need people to do it with unless you want to practice monologues. For most actors, the majority of it is done in two places, the audition room and on set, both of which don't give you a lot of reps.

Boxers talk about ring rust, that no matter how much you train, how much sparring or weight lifting you accomplish, nothing is a substitute for time in the ring. So if you go a year or more between fights, you're asking for trouble, your body has to readjust. Being able to act every day playing different characters and coming up with ideas was sharpening my weapons, it was allowing me to stay loose instead of how out of shape I would get between jobs.

At about this time I started getting offers to do college appearances as well.

Spoiler alert: people in college tend to consume inordinate amounts of social media, so being reintroduced to them put me on the short list to speak at these fine institutions. I hadn't done stand-up in years, but I was able to hobble together an act from stories throughout my career, plenty of *Drake & Josh* anecdotes, I knew what the people wanted. Plus there was this brand-new career I'd found myself in and it was incredibly topical considering that the profession of "influencer" was becoming more and more attractive to anyone with a smartphone. Thirty minutes of stand-up, thirty minutes of moderated Q and A with sometimes twenty-five hundred promising young minds clamoring to hear what I had to say. Weird.

Throughout all this, I was still auditioning, because, as I said, it's what I do.

Never once did I think, while I was busy being successful in this one area, that I would ever blow off an opportunity to act. The goal was the same, I was just taking a pit stop to gather some resources, and if anything, I enjoyed auditioning more because I was less desperate. It was less painful now and I was sharper because I spent most of my days in character—acting. It wasn't *Hamlet* but I was loose, I was getting reps in daily, and I could feel the effects.

I guess others felt the effect too because in April 2015 I booked a TV show. After almost two years of not working as an actor, I booked something, something big. This was a network TV show starring John Stamos and, well, me. This was my reintroduction, my chance to prove myself again—it was time for me to walk out on that stage as an adult and say, I deserve to be here—watch what I can do.

What a difference eighteen months makes, huh? I'd made it! I'd broken free of the old constraints and uncovered a whole new way to make a living. I was finding relevance in ways I'd never had, even when I was on TV every week, and the best parts were the ancillary effects it was having on my life. I could take a deep breath for the first time, knowing I didn't have to take whatever gig came my way, my mom was going to be okay, and I could progress in my life, maybe even marry my girlfriend.

But most importantly, I booked a TV show, a fucking network TV show. I was back, baby, I was back.

14

Adapt or Die

The show got canceled.

It was all looking so good, wasn't it?! Let's start with the show.

It was called *Grandfathered* and it ran for one glorious season on Fox between 2015 and 2016. I played John Stamos's son, which is ironic considering what I looked like from eleven through nineteen. I wish I could time-travel to thirteen-year-old chubby Josh and tell him, "One day we're going to be able to pass for John Stamos's offspring, so don't worry so much, and also put down that fifth slice of pizza while you still can."

I remember the process of auditioning for the show, each call-back, getting closer and closer, hearing that it was looking good but also thinking, *This is where they figure out I'm not right, I don't book jobs like this.* The last audition, I sat in a waiting room with three other guys that looked like me, all of us praying it was our turn for a yes. They called my name, I entered a dark theater with fifteen studio executives watching, staring, their faces obscured by the dark . . . I stood there, as I have hundreds of times, performing my lines, singing for my supper.

When I finished, I walked to my car and thought, *What just happened in there?* But before I got to the garage, my phone rang with a call from an unknown number. I picked up and heard the voice of John Stamos and the producers screaming, "CONGRATULATIONS!" Holy shit, I got it, I actually got it. This is the moment actors live for, truly, because once the excitement of getting the job wears off, the terror of actually *doing* the job sets in. But for those twenty-four glorious hours of knowing you beat everyone else, there's just nothing like it. It's the swings, baby! It's like being a gambling addict: you know you're going to spend most of your life losing but it's those wins, those rare wins that keep ya goin'.

I remember meeting John Stamos at the final audition. He looked at me and said with a wink, "My nieces like those videos you make. Think you can be funny for more than six seconds?" It was a good joke and also made me think, *Uncle Jesse has seen my Vines?* No, what it really made me think was, *Maybe these past two years brought me to this moment, maybe this social media following I had built truly was attractive to the people who made the decisions, maybe I'd given myself that edge that had always eluded me.*

I'd broken the spell, I was back—it took me six years and basically creating a whole new career for myself, but I was back and this time I wasn't going to let it slip away. I remember calling my agent and manager, my girlfriend, my mom, telling them the good news. Everyone was elated, they'd seen me through the tough times, the uncertainty, the constant self-doubt, and they were just happy to cross Josh off their list of things to worry about. I think for a month straight every time I got on the phone with my mom she'd end the call by saying, "I'm just so, so proud of you." Ugh.

I was back in the saddle for the first time on a network TV show, there was a billboard half a mile from my apartment with my face on it. I was excited to act again but I was equally excited to no longer have to hang my head when someone would ask, "What have you been up to?" The question "What have you been up to?" is kryptonite for an actor, especially when nothing's been "up." I was tired of going into a twenty-minute explanation of what Vine was as people wondered why I was now acting for my iPhone and not on television. Oh, I had something going on, something BIG. Unlike Vine, no one asked what Fox was.

But with all this excitement, all this possibility in the air, I was still on guard, still waiting for the other shoe to drop. It's like getting back with an ex who cheated on you: you're always going to check their phone. I was ecstatic to have this big, fancy job, to hopefully prove everyone who doubted me wrong, but I was still diligent when it came to the new social media business I had created. I couldn't devote as much time to it, but there was no way I was going to stop. I was too jaded, too ready for everything to hit the fan.

Whether between takes or before and after work, I was creating content. Making Vines, feeding Instagram, making long-form Facebook videos. I knew that to lose the momentum of what I'd created would be to turn my back on the thing that took care of me when nothing else did.

But I also enjoyed having a key card that opened the gate of a major studio, waving to security guards who recognized me as I drove in, and getting to wake up every day and get paid to act. Five percent of Screen Actors Guild members are able to make a living solely from acting. Five percent! I'd pull up to the studio every morning and think, *Am I one of those people? The lucky ones?*

I was, I actually was.

Why didn't I feel that way?

Here's why.

The show premiered to pretty good numbers and then never rose to those numbers again, each week falling a little bit in the ratings. It was a good show, and the people who loved it really loved it. I was proud to be part of it, but unfortunately it was just a precarious time in network television, the audiences were shrinking, and blah blah blah, it just didn't work.

As we edged toward our final few episodes, people in the crew kept saying, "See you next season!" I remember thinking, *No, you won't!* As the season finale was airing I was meeting my friend in Las Vegas for a yearly trip we take, and I knew that unless we had some spectacular showing, we were done for. I got the call on my way home from the airport from the creator of the show, and in that moment I got to be part of the long legacy of people who've had a show canceled.

It was weird because as I got the news, I remember this feeling washing over me. It wasn't frustration or anger, it wasn't relief, it was weirder than that. It was . . . familiar? Like, *Oh, I know what this feels like, of course this has happened, this tracks.* It was pragmatic on one hand and perhaps overly cynical on the other. I don't know, I just knew the data wasn't in our favor. If a major network picks up a dozen pilots every year, they're liable to order four of those to series, and maybe one or two of those shows will get a second season. I mean, by those standards we got pretty damn far, but when it was done, it was done.

Either way, it was back to the chopping block, back to auditioning, back back back. Back to my old neighborhood, struggle town—population, me. Being too successful for too long never suited old JP, I prefer the feeling of existential dread nipping at my heels anyway. Luckily, it was all tempered by the fact that I had a whole other business to rely on.

For the first time in my life, I had a contingency plan.

Scott Galloway, marketing professor at NYU and author of the book *The Algebra of Happiness*, talks about this exact scenario. He says, "Assume you're not Beyoncé. Assume that perhaps your overflowing wealth of talent will not be met with the perfect alchemy of luck and handwork that will combust into making you the biggest star in the world. Of course go for your dreams, but also nurture skills that are inherent to you, what are your super powers?"

Basically what I think Scott is saying is, there's nothing wrong with going for your dream. Hell, I've been doing it my entire life. But it's important to also nurture skills that can benefit you if statistically your dreams don't quite pan out. So if you find yourself with a great singing voice but also, by chance, are awesome at, let's just say, spreadsheets, don't be afraid to cultivate that talent too. Because by-products of a good job—say, as an accountant—are family and stability, which can also bring about comparable levels of happiness to achieving your dream. Okay, maybe not comparable, but you can have a nice life.

If Scott is right, and let's suppose he is—I mean I just devoted two paragraphs to him—I was sort of already doing this. First by getting sober, which had set me on a path of growth that required me to build a life not solely based on achievements. It didn't limit my ambition but it put into perspective the idea of how much I could get from it. Each meeting I went to, each estimable act I tried, was an attempt to fortify my resistance. I wanted to be a full person with a real life, but I knew that show business alone couldn't provide me with that.

When I finished filming the show, I asked Paige to marry me. I wasn't going to let this hiccup stop me from proposing to the woman of my dreams, and I had saved up more than enough scratch for a very decent engagement ring. I just didn't want my life going forward to be solely based on making it, I had lived that trap before and knew how depressing it could be. I wasn't even sure of what "making it" meant anymore, I just knew I had to keep living, keep growing, avoid the holding pattern.

I was back to my grind, going full speed as an actor, auditioning for everything and anything I could while also continuing to build my social media business. I had a wedding to pay for! All through 2016 I continued to work with brands, collaborate with other creators, create content, and hope that the next audition would be the game changer that would absolve me of all of it.

I know what you're thinking, I was handling all this surprisingly well. No neurotic, self-loathing spinouts here, baby! No running to a bar to drown my sorrows in whatever sugary drink had the highest alcohol content. I took the disappointments on the chin and just kept going, undeterred, let's go, Joshy Boy, don't let 'em keep ya down!

And then Twitter decided to discontinue the Vine app.

A total of 9.5 million followers, gone in an instant.

Shit.

And you wonder why I have trust issues? Shit. Shit. Shit. Shit.

It'll go down in the annals of business schools everywhere, the case study of the massive gaffe that was Vine's demise, but it doesn't matter. I'm not here to cast stones, I'm grateful for all it gave me, but 9.5 MILLION FOLLOWERS DOWN THE DRAIN.

Now what?

TV show? **Canceled.** Side hustle? **Canceled.**

What do I do now? Turns out being on a television show no one watched didn't give me the pop I was hoping for, so I was back to square one as an actor, and now the anchor of my social media business was rapidly trying to pull down the entire boat. I'd have to make a change and fast. I had been balancing both worlds pretty well, but with Vine gone I would have to pivot.

I couldn't rely solely on Instagram or Twitter; those weren't my platforms, and I didn't have the kind of following there that could command the money I was making on Vine. I needed somewhere new where I could make funny videos, and there was only one place to do it . . . YouTube.

Yikes.

The next and really only move was to create longer-form videos on YouTube, but this required an entirely different level of commitment, which is why I had avoided it. These weren't six-second videos shot on my phone, these were long-form content shot on professional cameras with hours of editing. It easily had the highest workload of any social medium, but it also had the biggest upside.

Rumors of million-dollar partnerships and sponsorships were starting to become more and more ubiquitous in the world of YouTube, but what was most attractive was the Google AdSense model. Google realized early on that YouTube was the most symbiotic of environments; they were nothing without the creator and vice versa, so they decided then to cut them in.

Basically what that meant was, every time you skipped through an ad for Starbucks before a YouTube video, the creator of that video made money. The rate can range from a dollar to ten dollars per a thousand views, so if your video got a million views, for example, and the rate was five dollars on that particular day, you would make five thousand dollars.

If you were successful on YouTube, you no longer had to hope some massive brand came by and asked you to work for them; the harder you worked, the better it paid. If you posted a video every other day with an average of half a million views per video, you could easily start seeing upward of $100k a month in AdSense revenue.

Real money, real security, but fuck! I just figured out this other thing, this Vine thing, and that was a fluke in itself; now I gotta figure out YouTube?! I have to pivot again?! I just pivoted, I'm fresh off a pivot! Adapt or die, I suppose. It was the obvious next step if I wanted to keep this train moving, and I did; the incentive was more than there, and the only child in me just wanted to keep having people to make jokes with.

But the optics were troubling. By this time the whole world was on social media, from Kylie Jenner to your Aunt Diane. It was weird if you didn't have a presence, but the only people on YouTube were . . . YouTubers. There was a definite distinction, and making that leap would be a clear sign that I was doubling down on social media, taking it really seriously. But what if I didn't get another job soon? How long before people stopped seeing me as an actor and started seeing me for whatever I was becoming? What if they stopped thinking of me altogether?

I don't know, I didn't have control over what people thought, but at a time when I had just been handed another massive L by show business, I didn't hate the idea of creating more content on my own. Again I had gone back to my ex and again I was shown the door. Figure it out yourself, Peck!

If I must. But where to begin?

The learning curve for YouTube was drastically more difficult than for Vine, which required only a phone and an idea. Nevertheless, I dove in, I bought the right camera, the right lens, the right editing software. I reached out to people on YouTube with big followings, I reverse engineered it. I tried to re-create all the elements that worked during my first foray into social media and apply them to this next chapter. I knew I'd get some eyes on it because I could drive audiences from my other platforms, but I also knew that they'd only stay if the content was good.

Jerry Seinfeld said when he went back to comedy after almost a decade of starring in the number one sitcom on television, "You get five minutes, five minutes of grace when they know and love you already. They'll give you a standing ovation, they'll laugh just because, but after five minutes, if you're not funny. They don't care who you are."

It was around this time I met one of the biggest creators on the platform, David Dobrik. Through friends, he invited me one day to shoot a bit he had come up with, and knowing he was such a prolific force on the platform I said yes. Pretty quickly, I started to spend time with David and his group of friends, who included people like Liza Koshy and others who had massive social media followings. As a thirty-year-old guy about to get married, I was positively geriatric compared to these twenty-one-year-old basically college students with a gigantic audience and comparable bank accounts.

I would recur in videos and, much like I did with Vine, try to pick up through osmosis the tricks of the trade, how to shoot, edit, and optimize videos. The art of "clickbait," figuring out provocative titles for videos so they got the most views possible. My friend Casey Neistat once said, "If you spend time making a video you're proud of, why wouldn't you use clickbait to make sure people actually watched it?"

For months I would shoot footage and do nothing with it, I was terrified to face it, to have to sift through the hours of footage and construct a narrative. I would shoot with friends who would say, "Do you just watch this footage alone in your room, Howard Hughes style? What are you doing with all this?" I didn't know, I was just trying to get my reps in, to be around the process till eventually the right path revealed itself because maybe Stamos was right, maybe I was only funny six seconds at a time.

That's how I spent the first six months of 2017. If I didn't have an audition to prepare for, I was shooting content that went nowhere. I didn't pressure myself, I knew more would be revealed if I just kept creating—even if no one saw it.

But by June of 2017 I had something more important to focus on. A wedding. That's right, Paige was making an honest man of me, and I was busy helping her with all the plans leading up to the big day, and by that I mean just trying to stay out of the way. But it occurred to me, as I was testing food and trying on suit jackets, that the days leading to a wedding might be really interesting to watch. Especially if the person getting married was someone you grew up with.

This became the thesis for my first video, "I GOT MARRIED!!!" I mean, what could be a more clickbait-rich title than that? Everyone is obsessed with celebrity weddings and this was the next best thing, an almost-celebrity wedding!

I wound up filming the days leading to the wedding, my groomsmen and I trying on our suits, the rehearsal dinner, my sister-in-law trying to talk me out of marrying her sister (don't ask), and edited it together into a seven-minute masterpiece of iMovie perfection. I included some other footage I had shot over the past few months and had my wife sign off on it, making sure I caught her at all the proper angles, and hit upload. Here goes nothing.

The video did well, really well, a million plus views well. I was off and running, nothing could stop me! Until my next video, which did half of that, and the next, which did half of that, until I was making weekly videos that were averaging fewer than a hundred thousand views. This was a problem, a real problem, because the workload was not small. There were more than a few times I got the look from my wife that said, "You're really pulling your camera out now?" Or "Maybe you could pry yourself from the edit and spend some time with me." I was militant, posting a video every week to less than tepid reactions. At that point tepid would have been a goal, this was pitiful.

Fifty-two weeks, fifty-two videos—all shit. I should've changed the name of my channel to "I'm trying my best!" I don't know why I kept going, except that I had literally nothing else going on. It had now been more than a year since I had booked an acting job, so in reality, if I wasn't focused on this, the only thing to think about was the abyss. Don't get me wrong, I loved being newly married and I still had some money coming in, but it felt like I was stalling out. I had to crack this new platform.

So what was wrong? Why couldn't I crack this thing? Should I just give up? In reality, it took me one full year of making videos to come to terms with the fact that I was wholly uncomfortable with the way I was going about it.

For a full year I was a fraud, I was doing my best impression of what I thought a YouTuber was, or more specifically, carrying my camera wherever I went, shoving it in friends' faces, creating pretend scenarios, and overall not being myself. I just couldn't be that guy who talked to his camera in public, it made me deeply uncomfortable, and the audience could tell.

The biggest and most constant note I've received from my wife throughout the years has been "Be yourself." She's an Apostle too, just don't tell her that.

It was at this time that a friend and collaborator of mine, my editor, my podcast cohost, and authority on all things internet, Joe Vulpis, said something to me that completely altered my YouTube career's trajectory.

"Why don't you try being in front of the camera?"

What an idea. Of course I technically was in front of the camera, but I was also operating it and worrying about all the things I wasn't good at. Lighting and sound and this thing called "in focus" which people seemed to really care about. "Why don't you focus on what you're good at, being funny, and I'll hold the camera" Joe might as well have said, "Be yourself." Seems to be a recurring theme.

So I took his advice and thought, *What's an idea for a video that would feel the most natural, the most like myself, the most me?* I know what you're thinking . . . chicken wings, that's exactly right.

During this time, YouTube was seeing a massive rise in something called *mukbangs*, also known as eating shows.

It was initially created in South Korea for people to watch when they came home from work. The idea was that because it's such a hardworking culture, people got home late at night and had no one to eat with, but now they could eat with their favorite YouTuber. The videos consisted of someone eating some kind of food, usually something delicious, usually something that you wouldn't eat if you were on a diet per se, and usually a good amount of it. The person would just talk to the camera as they housed a gigantic bowl of noodles.

I thought, *I like to eat, people* know *I like to eat, I already have street cred as a former thicc boy, so it wouldn't be far-fetched for me to do something eating based.* It's why it's hard to trust a skinny chef, but I was easily a couple of cheat days away from three hundred again, so the world knew I was uniquely qualified. I set up the camera, ordered enough chicken wings to fill a duffel bag, and hit record. It was like I was sitting across from a friend at dinner, talking shit and eating something delicious, which to me is one of the holiest of activities. I cut the video down from an hour, leaving in what I thought were the best parts, and uploaded it. Let's see what happens.

What happened was five million people watched that video and then a few more million watched the next one and the one after that. They weren't all massive hits, of course, but suddenly I was getting consistent viewership instead of the hit-or-miss record I had before. My channel within a year jumped from 500k followers to 1 million and then a year later to 3.7 million. The theme of the channel became mostly food-based; it was a ripe category, one that I was good at and that had unlimited possibility. It seemed as though the mass public spent most of their time fantasizing about food, and if they couldn't eat it themselves, they'd happily watch me do it.

Eventually I branched out to other experience-based videos. I tried the hottest chicken in the world with my friends Joe and Nick, I went to Taco Bell headquarters and tried new menu items that weren't released yet, Joe and I had our fat frozen off at a medical spa and the next day survived on only vending machine food for twenty-four hours. My channel became an "idiot's guide to fulfillment." I had a famous Realtor give me a tour of a fifty-million-dollar Bel Air mansion, I ate everything The Rock does on his cheat day. The idea was always *you* weren't going to do these things, but I could do them for you.

Between 2017 and 2019, my channel grew exponentially, as did all my other social media as by-products. Soon YouTube was my primary platform for creating and I was using it as an aggregate to send people to whatever I wanted to promote—podcast, merch, anything. The kinds of audiences on YouTube were unusually dedicated because they knew that the content being created took work.

Everyone can take a good photo, everyone can slap enough filters and Facetune on something till it looks cute, but a twenty-minute video that holds people's attention? That's a different story. It just requires a different level of dedication, and the audience appreciated the sweat.

I had a good system set up. I was filming almost every day, Joe with his lightning-fast edits would turn the videos over in twenty-four hours, and it became a machine. Just like when Rami told me to make a Vine every day, once I figured out the algorithm, I didn't deviate. I threw myself fully into YouTube and I didn't miss a week of posting for three years, even if that meant missing a family dinner or sitting in a hotel room editing while on vacation (sorry, Paige). This, like every other thing I've done, felt like there was a ticking clock to it. I knew it couldn't last forever but as long as it was working, I wasn't going to waste a second.

I was in a good groove, working, creating, maybe not in the way I was used to, but in a whole new way that challenged me to develop other skills. I learned how to edit, which went against every lazy impulse I'd ever had; I started to pick up on camera angles because I didn't have a director of photography to make sure I didn't miss anything; I learned how to give variations of performance so I wasn't locked into one version in the edit. YouTube was sort of my unofficial film school. It just rounded me out in a way I'm not sure I would've gained otherwise.

Soon, I wasn't the guy from Vine anymore, I was the guy from YouTube.

On any given day it was neck and neck on what some stranger might bring up to me, maybe it was "I loved that episode of *Drake & Josh*," or maybe it would be "Oh my

God, your YouTube video when you told all your friends that you and your wife were pregnant is my favorite."

You're probably thinking, *That's great, Josh, you were still relevant, people watched your stuff.* That's a completely rational thought; unfortunately, I am not a completely rational person. This was not "great." The reality was, things *were* going well, but it wasn't the kind of well I wanted.

I wanted to rip out my fucking eyeballs, in fact. I didn't want to be known as the "YouTube" guy, my fears were being realized, and they were completely of my own making. Even if I enjoyed it, even if I was proud of the videos, what I couldn't stand were the comments, which had become:

> **Twitter:** Where did Josh Peck go? **Reply:** He's a YouTuber now.
> **Twitter:** Yikes.

Can you blame me?! I could do my best here to try to save my image, to tactically and strategically word this next paragraph to make it look like I wasn't being an ungrateful dick, but I was. Social media success isn't some consolation prize, I know that. I was succeeding in something that is the goal for many people, I wasn't just surviving, I was *living*, in a way that acting never allowed me because I just didn't make consistent money doing it.

But I couldn't handle it. Every day that I grew on YouTube was another day spent not as an actor and further solidifying this new image of myself. Social media was cute when it was my side hustle, but when it was the only thing I had going, well, that was different.

Remember, this was still during YouTube's renaissance, before the traditional world had fully embraced it, before people realized that you could make enough money on YouTube to buy a small country, before Will Smith and Kevin Hart and Jack Black were like "Ya, sign me up." The assumption among the public was, if you once had a career in TV and movies and now you were eating hot chicken with your friends for views on YouTube, something went wrong.

Something went very wrong. People who were successful on YouTube used it as a springboard to get into movies and television, not the other way around.

I noticed that I had become lazy as an actor too. I mean it's incredible how a safety net can sabotage you if you let it. I just wasn't putting the same level of commitment in that I had previously. There were fewer and fewer auditions where I walked out feeling like I had truly nailed it, and more where I just felt "meh." I was never unprepared, but it was hard to devote the hours it required when I knew I could spend that time making a video that would instantly net me a couple grand. The problem was, the people who were beating me out for the jobs *were* devoting that time to it. I was being outworked and I knew it.

I was having a full existential crisis. These are the worst

kinds of pitiful, literal First World problems, crying with two loaves of bread under my arms, and I'm pretty sure it was brioche. I was ashamed, I'll be honest. Every time someone commented something shitty on YouTube, I wanted to write back, "Don't you know that I was in a movie that won Sundance that no one saw?! Don't you know that Bryan Cranston wasn't respected till he was like fifty and that's all I have to hold on to?!"

It's so ugly, I'm not proud of it, but this is my truth, dear reader, and if I can't be honest with you, who can I be honest with? My therapist? No thanks!

I had become a victim of my own success, of my need for security. On one hand, I had done everything right, I had leaned into something that was working, really working. It wasn't easy by any means, but I took advantage of an opportunity, of timing and luck, and started something that grew into this real thing. But maybe I leaned in too far? Maybe I didn't have to be posting multiple videos a week on multiple platforms, collaborating with other creators, taking every and any opportunity that came my way. I didn't know how to do it differently; I'm not known for moderation, as we know.

This was also a time when I watched people I had worked with, people like David, facing controversy and succumbing to the pressure that came with having to push the envelope with every new video (and the inevitable disasters that ensued). What would keep people's attention? What would keep them tuning in? Thankfully, between being married, sober, and with a kid on the way, I was too anchored, plus I had gone through my own period a decade earlier of being young and supremely stupid. But it was enough to make me question if I was going to keep creating, was this how I still wanted to do it? Or did I want to do it how I had always done it, as an actor, the way that made me happiest?

There's another word for an overblown need for security and that word is "greed." I'd become greedy. Because I had security, I had been okay for a while now, not Rolls-Royce megamansion security, but more than enough to take care of me and my family. When my wife would say something like, "If you're frustrated with where you're at as an actor, why don't you back off the social stuff? You're good, we're good, maybe take a break and focus on what's important to you?" I would reply, "Not if you like that Tesla you're driving!" I'm kidding, I didn't say that because I like being married, but I would say, "I can't let off the gas, we don't know how long this will last. If I take a break now, there's no telling if I'll be able to recapture this."

Scared of what would happen if I stopped and scared of what would happen if I kept going, that's never a good place to be. I was thirty years old and on the precipice of not so young anymore. If I was going to make one more run at this thing, I'd have to do it now. I'd have to pivot . . . again. Ugh.

15

Begin Again

For the last section of this book, I want to focus on the two most recent and important pivots in my life over the past three years. Moments I can track that directly influenced where I am today. I figure because they are so recent and impactful, it would behoove us to really look at them, as they led me to this book and so much more.

Here's the first:

There's something I didn't mention about *Grandfathered*, the show I made for Fox with John Stamos. Here goes: I didn't get good reviews for my performance in that show. Okay, strike that, they weren't all bad but there were definitely some people who were thoroughly unhappy with my performance. Okay, double strike that, most of the reviews were *highly* unfavorable when it came to my performance and I don't know why I'm trying to save myself here. Eventually, as the series went on, some of the critics came around, but that's not important; what *is* important is that *I* was unhappy with it. In fact, I'd been unhappy with my work for a while now, and I started to suspect that maybe *Red Dawn* wasn't a fluke, maybe I was just no good.

Let me be more specific. Over the past decade, since I did *The Wackness*, I had acted in four or five movies, a pilot, a season of television, a few guest stars, and there were definitely performances in there I'm proud of. One or two for sure. Definitely one. At least one. I think. The problem was lack of consistency. I could be really good or really not good. I was like a basketball player with no foul shot: it's cute you can dunk but eventually the other team will figure you out and foul you every time. Maybe my jump shot wasn't great either. Feeling *very* butch with all these sports references.

I know what you're thinking, *But Josh, you just mentioned all these things you worked on, how did you book them if you were bad?* Again, I *had* done good work before so I coasted off that, and I could usually get it together during the audition process—it was a scene or two that I had drilled for weeks—but when I actually got the job, I just had trouble seeing it all the way through. I was like an NFL player who crushed the combine but fell apart on game day, another sports reference, boo yah! I can recall when the trouble started.

A year after I made *The Wackness*, I auditioned for a film called *Remember Me*. I badly wanted this movie, it was well written, a New York story, and it was being cast by the same casting director as *The Wackness*. This was a layup: the producers liked me, I was right for the role, it was perfect. Guess we're going back to New York, baby, never been to Sundance sober, *let's do this*. I just had to go in there and not completely shank it.

I shanked it.

I remember the feedback from the audition was "His performance was overwrought." The *Oxford English Dictionary* defines "overwrought" as tense, agitated, nervous, on edge. It goes on to use words such as frantic, frenzied, hysterical, panicky. Now as a person, overwrought sounds like a perfectly appropriate characterization, but as an actor, it was less than ideal.

Remember, this was coming from a casting director who *liked* me. Can you imagine what she would have said if she didn't? Wasn't I good? I was good, right?

I remember another audition not long after that for a little show called *Boardwalk Empire*. The auspices were good, really good. Steve Buscemi as the lead, HBO, and Martin Scorsese producing? Uh yeah, I suppose I could make time for that. In fact, Scorsese's casting director, Ellen Lewis, renowned as one of the great casting directors of her generation, was casting the show and asked specifically to see me. ME. Well, of course she did, I was good! Right?

We exchanged small talk, she told me how much she liked *The Wackness*, I told her how much I liked every

movie she'd ever worked on, and then the audition began. After I was finished, Ellen paused and said, "Are you
studying with anyone?" Which was a nice way of saying,
"Are you in acting class? Because you should be." Remember what I said about Apostles not being afraid to hurt
your feelings?

Listen, I don't want to put words in people's mouths,
I don't know if that's for sure what she meant because I
never asked her, but of course that's what she meant. And
it was nice, it was a nice way of saying something without
exactly saying it. It was nicer than what most casting directors would have done, which is tell you "Thank you"
and then complain to your agent about what a train wreck
you were.

Looking back, it was clear. I needed to reassess, I
needed to look at what I was doing, shit was misfiring, the
sequencing was off, there was a bug in the system, but I ig-
nored it. I didn't have time to consider that I might not be
good, I had devoted my entire life to this thing, my mom
depended on it, my wife depended on it, *I* depended on it.
and the thought that perhaps I had been an impostor this
whole time with just really good luck, well, that was just
too much to handle.

The truth was, I wasn't an impostor—well, not completely. I *could* be good, in the right thing. Playing a drug
addict, hip-hop head, New York kid in *The Wackness*?
Not a stretch. Playing an overweight, nerdy, comically

broad, magic-loving kook in a show with my name in it, *not a stretch*. Certain parts would come up and I would kill them, but they were few and far between. And isn't acting about disappearing? Isn't it about transforming into a character that might be nothing like you?

I was like a fighter with a twenty-twenty record, lose that much and eventually it doesn't matter how many times you've won. "But I knocked out the champion of the world at Madison Square Garden?! Didn't you see me?" Yeah yeah, we saw you but right now you're losing to a bum in the ballroom of a Ramada.

I had a suspicion for too long that I had too many blind spots, too many bad habits, too many gaps in my knowledge, and after ten years of mixed feedback and feeling bad about what I was doing, there was enough data to validate it. If I ever wanted to be great or more specifically just work again, I'd have to humble myself, I'd have to truly look at my flaws and face the idea that maybe my best wasn't enough.

It's a scary prospect. So many people in life never give their all, they never completely give themselves over to something so that their ego has a safety net, an out, a secret assurance that if things don't work out, they can always tell themselves it's because they didn't try hard enough. I didn't have that luxury. If I sucked, I needed to know. Now.

Let's go back.

When I was fourteen and recently moved to Los Angeles, I had an audition for a one-hour drama called *Touched by an Angel*. The feedback from the audition was "Nice kid, can't act." I really wish that had been reversed, I would've much preferred the feedback had been "Kid's a douche but what an actor." Nevertheless, he was right. I had never been trained as an actor except in the art of make it as big and ridiculous as you can until people started laughing. Whatever version of acting I was doing was some Frankenstein creation I'd learned from doing stand-up and listening to my mom say, "Milk the joke, baby!" This was not great advice.

Thankfully my manager at the time had the foresight to say, "He needs to go to acting class or I'm not going to represent him anymore." An ultimatum, I like it! Who can blame her? I'm sure she didn't want any more calls from casting directors asking why she was wasting their time.

This is what brought me to my first acting class, Monday nights at 6:00 p.m. in a not-not-bad part of the San Fernando Valley with a guy named Andrew Magarian. In the class were twenty or so students, including Evan Rachel Wood, Mae Whitman, Penn Badgeley, Evan Peters. and Dakota Fanning. Heard of 'em? It was a murderers' row of young actors, people who took the craft incredibly seriously, and me . . . oh, boy.

I remember my first scene in class, I loaded up, got prepared, and thought, *Watch this shit*. I mean I was working; I was on *The Amanda Show*, I was getting *paid* to act, I had to be good, right? Of course I was, and it was time for me to show it.

Andrew stopped me after my first line—MY FIRST LINE—and said, "What are you doin'?" *Crushing it*, I thought. Andrew proceeded to have me perform the line over and over and over again until it had become almost nothing, until I was too exhausted to put any spin on it, any English, any shtick, and I just said it the way we say most things in life, without much effort at all. Andrew looked at me and said, "Good, now try the next line." And back around we went.

Most people can be critical because most people know when something doesn't work. You don't have to be a musician to know when someone hits the wrong note, you just have to have ears. But when someone can show you your mistakes and also help you fix them? Well, that's what makes a great teacher, and that's what Andrew was. I was hooked.

Over the next five years, I went to class every single week, I rarely missed. I learned how to act, how to listen, how to prepare for a scene, how to break down a script, and why it's important to put in the work because, as Andrew says, "As an actor, you're telling someone else's story, and you owe it to them to get it right." I got good—quickly. I had some natural talent, so once I was given the instruction manual on how to use it, I was off to the races.

It all culminated in *Mean Creek* and *The Wackness*, two movies that I was uniquely qualified for. Getting great reviews for my performances in those movies cemented the idea that I was good, *really* good, the best of a generation perhaps. I'm not kidding, and trust me I'm getting the same douche shivers you are. I thought I was brilliant and that my performance in *The Wackness* was but a preview of more to come, that my life would just be a nonstop orgy of incredible performances, awards, and idolatry for my prolific dopeness.

I didn't need class anymore, I just needed more opportunity to strut my stuff, let this race car out of the garage, baby! That was the beginning of the end for me looking back. The moment I thought there was nothing else for me to learn was the moment I arrested my development as an actor and began to acquire bad habits to bridge the gap for how quickly out of shape I would become. I was like a fat guy with a black belt, I figured I was set because I was good once.

Aaron Sorkin, when asked about his career in writing, said two things. The first was "Even a baseball player who strikes out two out of three times he goes up to bat will go to the Hall of Fame." He followed that with "Last night's meal won't keep you fed." It was the perfect analogous combination to sum up, in my opinion, the life of any artist. Keep on swinging because even someone with a losing record is still a winner, and you must stay vigilant. You must stay primed, you must stay fit for the activity you're trying to accomplish, be it in the gym or the boardroom.

Whenever people find out I'm thirteen years sober they ask, "You still go to meetings? Aren't you all better?" As if somehow a vaccine was administered. I heard a guy at a meeting once say, "If this was only about drinking too much, they'd round up every alcoholic from skid row to the Pacific Palisades, throw 'em in the lockup for thirty days, let 'em dry out, and then they'd never drink again."

Problem solved, right? Except it ain't about drinking, that's what you'll come to find out. Drinking was but a symptom of a greater problem that centered in my mind. And *that* problem required constant maintenance, constant vigilance, constant spiritual principles. Because my mind wants me dead and the only way to combat that is to have a daily practice.

You wouldn't second-guess Kobe Bryant when you heard that after a game, win or lose, he would put up five hundred free throws. When I interviewed Tim Grover, coach to Michael Jordan among others, he said, "After every single game, I would ask Michael one thing, 'Six, seven, or eight?' which meant 'What time are we hitting the gym tomorrow?'" It's assumed that to achieve excellence, you need that level of commitment, grit, work ethic to achieve a flow state when you're on the big stage. Nothing good in life can be maintained without practice.

Somehow, I had forgotten that, or maybe I never knew

it to begin with. I was doing my best impression of what I thought a good actor was without any of the work, I just wanted to be complimented again. For almost ten years, I was serving only myself and what I thought would make me look good, not the writing (which is your only job as an actor), not what the character required (which is your only job as an actor), not even what the director wanted (which is your only job as an actor . . . if the director is good), and it was landing me in a world of hurt. That was why I was trash in *Red Dawn*, that was why I felt like the wrong guy in *Grandfathered* and pretty much everything else I did during that time.

I would walk onto a set or to an audition praying that my talent would show up, praying that I could summon who I once was.

A stroke of luck befell me in 2015 when I was meeting my manager in New York City. I was working on a little independent movie there (Another half-realized, kind of good, kind of bad performance from old JP) and my manager said, "Hey, I know we're supposed to grab dinner tonight, but would you want to have dinner with me at my client Vincent D'Onofrio's house instead? He's having people over and said you could come."

Um, yes, I would love to break bread with one of our greatest living actors. I showed up at his house and sometime over the evening, completely unprompted, I asked Vincent if he knew of any good acting classes. Why? I have no idea, I was like a drunk asking where the good AA meetings were. He looked at me and said, "There's only one teacher who teaches real method acting the way it was originally taught. Her name is Sharon Chatten, she's my teacher. That's who you should go see."

I thanked him and then quickly filed that away in the deep recesses of my mind because I had years of bad acting left to do. It wasn't till two years later, when I was unemployed and in enough pain to do something about it, that I remembered that conversation. I called Sharon, set up a time to check out her class, and immediately felt that wave of relief you get when you complete an errand you've been pushing off for a decade.

A week later, I showed up at a black box theater in Venice. Sharon walked in, mid-sixties, sandals, comfortable clothes, with this sort of maternal energy about her. I introduced myself and she asked, "Who referred you again?" I responded, "Um, Vincent? Vincent D'Onofrio? I'm a big deal, remember?" "Oh, right!" she responded. "Why don't you watch the first half of class and then you can participate when we move on to scenes."

I watched as she began to put everyone through a relaxation exercise, people's shoulders began to lower, their bodies became loose, it was pretty incredible. Remember that quote of Lee Strasberg, "Fear and tension interrupts expression"? Well, this seemed like a good way to combat that, probably because he invented it.

Once that was over, it was time for my scene partner and me to do our scene, time for me to get up there and show my stuff. Oh, boy, I was worried, I'll be honest, again I was hoping—praying—that my talent would show up. But again, my ego also told me that since I had more credits than most of the people in the class, I should be fine. I told myself that lie, that lie I had been telling for a decade now, *I was good once, I should be good again.*

It would be the last time I'd ever think that.

Sharon stopped me after the first line that came out of my mouth. It was Groundhog Day and I was fourteen all over again. We proceeded to spend the next thirty minutes on that one line. ONE LINE. Do you know how utterly humiliating that is, to be sitting in a class of people staring at you, people who quite possibly grew up watching you on television, as a teacher dismantles everything you ever believed about yourself? Cutting down every bit of subterfuge and facade you've created to reveal the truth, which was "Oh, you don't actually know what you're doing, do you?"

The next week, I showed up to class, went through the relaxation exercise, and then it was time for my scene. Halfway through, Sharon stood and said, "Josh, who am I?" She then proceeded to walk around with her shoulders slumped, mimicking my awful posture. I hadn't realized that for years, because I had been so overweight, and then even after I got in shape, I had begun to hold my body in a way that closed it from view. I tried to minimize myself, rounding my shoulders, slouching over so that my shirt wouldn't hug the parts of my body I was still insecure about. I had been walking around with a hump in my back and closed off for ten years, wondering why I looked so weak all the time, so unconfident.

I wanted to kill her; actually I wanted to kill myself and then her.

Actually, I just wanted to kill myself. I went home that night breathless; I woke Paige up and told her what happened, I was having a full anxiety attack, my mind spinning from having someone so efficiently and strategically cut right to the root of me. I wasn't mad at her, I was reeling from being so seen, from immediately having the past decade flash before my eyes and thinking, *Why didn't I do this sooner?* It wasn't all as simple as pull your shoulders back, but still, why did I wait so long?

For the next six weeks when I walked into class, I couldn't even make it through an entire scene without her stopping me. It wasn't severe or cutting, it was brutal and honest. When I interviewed Gabby Reece for the podcast, she asked me if I wanted to do a pool workout before we recorded, a system of under- and above-water workouts with heavy weights that she and her husband, Laird Hamilton, had created. Of course I was game. Gabby and Laird being the physical specimens they are, I knew this would be special.

I reviewed an exercise with Gabby that would take me twelve feet down to the bottom of their pool, carrying a thirty-pound weight, and then swimming it to the surface. I remember her saying, "I'm going to speak to you very directly and clearly, making sure you understand what I'm saying. A lot of people can't take being spoken to like this, but this isn't yoga class. You could die underwater, it's important that I know you understand me." That's how Sharon spoke, it was tough and direct, she just wouldn't allow bad work.

Each week I returned to class for my shellacking, but each week I would learn new concepts and techniques about method acting. The same techniques created by Konstantin Stanislavski, as taught to people such as Lee Strasberg and Harold Clurman, who then taught them to people such as Al Pacino, Sidney Poitier, and Paul Newman and famous teachers like Sharon. It all seemed so simple, acting was no longer this amorphous, ephemeral thing, this alchemistic practice that could only be summoned by the truly elite. It was pragmatic, it was like anything, here are the basics, learn them completely, and then build upon that foundation. Somehow I had gotten this far without learning them.

I remember one week, after a particularly tough class where it felt like I wasn't making any progress, I got a call from Sharon. Being keyed into her students the way she was, perhaps she could sense that I was losing faith. She said, "You've worked a lot, so you don't like to be bad at things. That can be hard for students like you. But here's what I can tell you, class is where you want to fail, class is where you want to stretch, so you can be free in front of the camera. In front of an audience. I've seen famous actors come to The Actors Studio, put up something completely out of their wheelhouse, *Hamlet* or something, and leave in tears but also feeling brave and inspired." She was right: I hated not being good, it brought up every fear I'd ever had about myself, my weaknesses, my bad habits, my lack of talent. It hurt, but I knew I needed it.

About three months into class, I put up a scene one night that Sharon didn't interrupt. In fact, I remember the last line of the scene leaving my lips and thinking, *Oh my God, we made it through.* The lights of the theater turned on and my scene partner and I waited nervously for our feedback. "That was so fucking good." She loved it, she loved it. I walked home that night on a cloud, gliding down the street, which is not a rare occurrence in Venice. It was like the glimmer of a lighthouse after a night of rough seas. The scene worked because I had incorporated everything I'd learned thus far, this shit was working. Three months might not sound like a long time to get better at something, but it is when you've been making a living doing it for almost twenty years. It's a goddamn eternity.

Since then, I haven't stopped working with Sharon,

either through private coaching or group classes. I know why I felt like an impostor my whole life, because, to put it simply, I wasn't doing the work and honestly, for years I didn't even know what the work was. I had succeeded through some natural talent and good direction early on but that was too random, too unreliable.

Here's what I now know: I know I'm not as gifted as some actors out there, that when God was handing out fistfuls of talent, he might have spent more time on Tom Hardy. And in the looks department as well; damn it, he's gorgeous. But I know this too, I now know how to do the work, how to prepare, how to honor what the writer wants and what the story requires. I've had a taste of what the great teachers taught, I've done scenes from the great plays, from the great writers. I have a framework and a foundation from which good work can be born. I'm in shape and ready to do my job to the best of my ability.

I wasn't a fake, I wasn't an impostor anymore.

16

You're the Fish You're Trying to Catch

I was sitting in a speaker meeting once, which is a twelve-step meeting with one speaker who talks for about forty-five minutes. Most meetings are like the ones you see in movies, someone speaks for ten to fifteen minutes and then there's open sharing for the remainder. Speaker meetings tend to attract people with a strong pitch, someone who has a long story and has gotten good at telling it. Someone who after ten minutes doesn't get flustered about what to say next.

It was in that meeting that I heard something I have never forgotten, it was a harbinger of what was to come. I was listening as this woman in her fifties was speaking from a lectern to a hundred or so people, but she might as well have been talking directly to me.

"Let me ask you this, what are you willing to let go that stands between you and happiness? The obvious stuff is easy, that anger you've been holding on to, that resentment. But what about the things you think are assets? That relationship you think you can't live without, that job you think defines you, can you let go of that? Because, if you're really serious about getting happy, you might be forced to let it all go, to know you can be okay without it. Because you're the fish you're trying to catch, you are the love of your life, you're everything you've been searching for."

I remember sitting there, riveted, and thinking, *She is so right.* And in the next breath thinking, *God, I hope that doesn't happen to me.*

Let me tell you where I was in the fall of 2019.

My social media business was netting seven figures a year with no sign of slowing down, my wife was still thoroughly in love with me for some reason, we bought a house and then pulled out at the last minute because the people were crooks but we eventually did buy a house, and most importantly, I was crushing being a dad.

My son was nine months old, and becoming a father came as natural to me as anything I'd ever done. I'd seen friends struggle, guys who said they didn't feel a connection with their baby until they could swing a bat or throw a ball. I feared I'd be the same, wondering if I'd be good at it. I had no role model, no training, and yet somehow it was second nature. I just liked it.

I found every moment enjoyable, from the sleepless nights to the never-ending walks pushing his stroller as he slept, I got a kick out of the most mundane tasks. Even when he got his first ear infection, I remember giving his name to the pharmacist, not believing I had helped create this person, Max Peck, who now had his own account at CVS.

I was married to the love of my life, the perfect person for me. Meeting Paige felt like a cosmic penance for the first twenty-four years of my life. It was as if the universe said, "He's a good kid and all he has is his mom, throw him a family already, it's time." I had found someone perfectly suited for me, someone so effortlessly kind, loyal, and smart that even my most neurotic of episodes couldn't dissuade her.

Unbeknownst to me, I had become someone worth loving; I know what you may be thinking, that everyone is worth loving. Well, that may be true, but certainly not everyone is capable of attracting the kind of partner they want to be loved by. I remember hearing at an AA meeting, when looking for a sponsor, "pick a guy who has what you want." Now, that didn't mean pick a guy with a Ferrari, although I'm not sure I could trust a guy in Rollerblades. It meant pick someone who had the life you want.

I used this same logic when Paige and I started dating, and all throughout our relationship, anytime we had a fight or I was unsure of what to do next, I consulted a married friend, someone whose relationship I respected. Whereas my single friends would give my sage advice such as "Hold your ground, bro" or "You can't let her get the upper hand," my married friends would say "Did you try apologizing?" or "Just try not to do anything to make it worse and it'll pass." Sound advice, advice I knew was good because it came from people in the thick of it, people actually *in* relationships. As a point, be wary of people who freely try to advise you about something they have no experience in.

Paige and I in many ways are the epitome of opposites attracting. This Irish Catholic girl from Sacramento, one of four from a family of educators, doctors, and football players, marries this hot-blooded Jew from a family of headhunters and dental floss magnates. Deep down, though, we're very alike, both artists, both with an affinity for French cinema and Asian cooking, but like any great partnership, being with her revealed to me all the things I never knew I needed.

Paige taught me how to stick around when the going got tough, she taught me the true meaning of family, that no matter what, family doesn't leave. You could get in fights, you could be imperfect, you could even go to bed angry. It didn't matter because family doesn't leave; we could figure this out right now or a week from now but it doesn't change the fact that I'll be here when we do. This was new information for me, I had never felt this level of unbridled loyalty from anyone. It was nice.

A friend of mine in sobriety once told me, "Be careful how much growing you do alone. A lot of people become these Fabergé eggs, perfectly pristine, detailed, and ornate, but the second you throw them around a little, they shatter.

Once you get a year sober, get busy helping others; that's the only way you'll continue to grow, by seeing your own humanity through the lens of other people and how you affect them.

That's what I had, with Paige, with our son, Max, and the people who were closest to me, real relationships. I was almost thirty-three and as I looked around, I had a community of people both close and extended who respected me, who knew they could count on me and I could count on them.

The Greek philosopher Heraclitus said, "Your character is your fate." My life was a reflection of character I suppose because, despite my misgivings, despite my still neurotic nature, my affinity for feeling like an impostor, the wreckage I'd once created, and the trauma of things outside my control, my life was that of a good man. Perhaps trying my best to do the right thing over and over had resulted in the life I had always wanted.

A good life as the result of good living.

In November 2019, I was in the best place, financially, I'd ever been.

Transitioning full tilt into the YouTube space in 2017 turned out to be a worthy cause because 250 "SHUA VLOGS" later, I achieved that goal of making six figures a month from Google AdSense. In a little under three years,

I grew my channel to 3.7 million followers, my Instagram to more than 10 million followers, and had secured multiple brand sponsorships every month across all platforms. Rami was right, social media was the future and I had pivoted just in time to take full advantage of it.

I was doing more than a dozen speaking engagements a year, speaking at different colleges all over the country, racking up frequent flyer miles, and doing preliminary surveys of where Max will eventually go to school. This assuming, of course, that I let him move away one day, which, as I write this sentence, is not likely.

I had created the *CURIOUS* podcast and interviewed 120 people I look up to, people I've mentioned and more, from John Stamos to Laird Hamilton, Ryan Holiday, Robert Greene, Daymond John, Dan Fogelman, Nick Bilton, Pete Berg, Gabby Reece, and Nikki Glaser. When guests would ask why I started *CURIOUS*, I would tell them, "Because if I had just asked you to lunch, you probably would've said no. Somehow entering microphones into this scenario makes it mutually beneficial." I was getting a chance to pick the brains of some of the most impressive people, people whose wisdom I could mine and one day share in a book just like this.

So that was November 2019.

I had a wife and child who loved me and I loved them. Among YouTube, brand integrations, speaking engagements, and the podcast, I had four different income streams, all producing a healthy amount of money each month. I was always busy, creating content every day, chasing down interview requests for the podcast, and traveling twice a month for different speaking engagements. I was okay, my mom was okay, we weren't going to be poor anytime soon, and we'd never have to go back to New York again. I was sober eleven years and weighed 180 pounds; okay, 190. My life was full.

"Okay, Josh, enough burying the lead, we know you too well by now, drop the hammer already, and tell us what was wrong," the reader said to themselves.

Here's what was wrong.

Sometime, over the three year span between November 2016 and November 2019, I stopped working as an actor. When I say stopped working, I mean exactly that. I didn't work at all, it was the longest span I'd ever gone without booking a job, and there was no relief in sight. I never stopped auditioning, never stopped making it my number one priority, and yet somehow, it seemed, the business had moved away from me.

I came close a few times over those three years, tested for a few pilots, did a chemistry test with Dennis Quaid that I completely shanked because I was in such a state of fear about booking another gig. I was slightly distracted by the fact that he brought his dog to the audition as well, but for the record, Dennis Quaid was very nice and so was his dog, who had no business being there. I couldn't get a job for the life of me and it seemed as though all the goodwill I had accrued, all my past work experience, meant nothing. No one wanted what I was selling.

It was even worse because I *had* been in acting class the last three years, working on my skills, trying to get better. I knew from class that what I was doing was good or at least the best of my ability, that there were no more excuses, no more bad habits, so if me at my best still wasn't good enough? Well, that was terrifying. It validated my worst fear: what if my life, my success until this moment, was a fluke or all my good luck had just dried up? Had the whole world received a copy of my diary and agreed with what I really thought of myself?

As time went on, I stopped getting asked "What are you working on?" and started getting asked "Are you still acting?" People no longer introduced me as an actor and instead would introduce me as an "influencer" or "social media personality" or "what would you call those videos you make?" Trigger warning, of course there's nothing wrong with being an influencer or a creator, I am also those, and they're very legitimate and respectable ways to make a living. I'd just spent my entire life devoted to this other thing, this thing I loved so much, and it seemed like it was being erased from my history.

I got offered to be on *Dancing with the Stars*, the harbinger of death for any actor's career; I even flew to New York to do a brand integration with Lay's potato chips and was told, "We want to do a throwback theme for our chip campaign and you're the perfect throwback star." Ouch. Throwback star? I'm only thirty-two. When I got my first tattoo, I posted a photo of it on Instagram and one of the comments read, "Won't having tattoos get in the way of you getting acting roles? Oh wait, never mind." Sick burn, that one hurt. It's always the comments with a seed of truth that really get you.

During this time I went to audition for some television show; it was a pilot so they were auditioning multiple people that day for different parts. When I walked into the waiting room there were three kid actors, probably about twelve years old, waiting to audition. They all looked like I did at that age, perhaps they didn't possess the same heft, but I could recognize their eagerness from a mile away. Poor saps, if only they knew what they were signing up for. I remember signing in, sitting down, starting to go over my lines in my head when I saw one of the kids in my periphery trying to get my attention. Shit. When I walked in there, I knew these kids were prime *Drake & Josh* viewing age, there was a good chance they were watching reruns of the show that morning. I turned to the kid, he looked at me and said "What are *you* doing here?" Good question. Now, instead of thinking, *I'm an actor just like you and this is what we all do, there are plenty of stories of people far more accomplished than me who've had to audition for parts and I'm just continuing the long-standing tradition,* I thought, *Yeah, you're right, what AM I doing here?* It was like having twelve-year-old Josh staring at me and asking, "Wait, we're thirty-two and still auditioning? I thought we'd be past this." You and me both, kid, you and me both.

That was in April, and by November 2019 I was so bitter and disgusted with myself, with the business, with feeling like a flop, a has-been, a wash-up, a never was, that I alerted my agent and manager that I no longer wanted to audition anymore. After twenty years I just couldn't take it, the preparation, the nerves, the rejection. I was over it. It was my silent protest, I'll show that motherfucker of a business who's boss, I won't let it walk away from me, I'll walk away from it! My ego was running riot, doing whatever it could to protect itself, my pride was in the twelfth round and looking for a knockout.

There was no closure to it, nothing healthy about it, it was a fit. Like a six-year-old who grabs a change of underwear and tells his parents he's running away because they won't give him dessert. He's got nowhere to go, no plan, but he sure does feel powerful for the moment.

I want to talk about two capital T truths that were present for me at that time.

Here's the first.

The reason you're reading this book, the reason I have anything in my life, is because of acting. It has informed everything that has happened to me since I started when I was nine years old. It quickly went from a hobby to a full-blown profession in a few short years and it's been the thing that I have spent the most time doing. I'm proud of it, I'm grateful for it, I love it, I love doing it, I love watching it, I love being around it. It allowed me to escape my thoughts when I was a kid, it saved me from poverty, from New York, from myself. It gave me confidence when nothing else could.

There was nothing I could do about this truth, this truth was out of my control.

Here's the second one.

I *needed* you to like me. I was drowning in what other people thought of me. I deeply cared about what *you* thought—okay maybe not you because I imagine you're not hate-reading this book, but about the Twitter mob, the critics, the audience, and anyone I had ever encountered throughout my life. I cared about the stranger who approached me and said, "Why haven't I seen you in anything in a while?" The casting director who said, "Josh is great, he's just not right." My ego was in a full death knell, I was crushed, I just couldn't deal with the idea that people thought of me as a failure, a cliché, a once-was. It hurts even to write it.

This truth, though, I could do something about.

I knew something had to change and I was worried that despite how blessed I was, how good my life had become, that I'd always be unhappy as long as I continued to chase this thing. The wins were incredible, but the time in between was getting longer and more painful, I wanted to be there for my wife, for my kid, for life, and I didn't want it to be blighted by this thing I couldn't let go of.

But could I let it go? I would have to, I had no choice.

People let go of their dreams every day, right? College ballplayers who face the reality that this might be the last time they get to suit up, ballet dancers who leave conservatory and realize their body just can't keep up, but an actor's body never breaks down. There's no clear line that says, "It's enough already, hang it up." In acting, your career is over a year before you decide to quit, anyway.

So the idea that perhaps I wouldn't make it, that maybe, just maybe I was going to have to let go of this thing I loved so much, was crippling. I was locked in a state of indecision, I just didn't know what to do. It was like a pebble in my shoe, a wound that wouldn't heal. Every time I truly considered walking away, there was this nagging feeling, this voice in the back of my head, sometimes a scream, sometimes a whisper, but always there, telling me I had unfinished business.

"That relationship you can't live without, that job that you think defines you, what are you willing to let go of that stands between you and happiness?"

So that's where I was one rainy evening in December 2019, driving around Northern California by myself, thinking about my life and what to do. We had driven up north for the holidays to be with my wife's family and after the fourth day in a row of champagne toasts and cheese boards, I needed some time to think. Maybe I was reflective knowing the new year was upon us, maybe I was just beaten into a state of willingness for the fifth time in my life, but as I drove, I decided to call a friend in AA, as I'd learned to do when I felt out of sorts.

My friend Harris picked up, a guy I've known since I got sober, and someone I surely wouldn't be friends with if we were both drinking. He kind of scares me. I told him everything, everything I told you, focusing primarily on the important part, that I knew my life was good, that I didn't want to do anything to mess that up even if that meant letting go of this thing I loved so much.

Here's what he said:

"Josh, your life has been an anomaly. To have had the success you had at an early age is abnormal, you can't chase that shit, you can't compare yourself to where you were then.

"It took well into my thirties to figure out what the hell I wanted to do with my life, I even had to go bankrupt. So if you're telling me that at thirty-three you don't know what the fuck to do with your life, I would say you sound exactly where you're supposed to be."

Jesus. Oh, and if that wasn't enough, he went on to say,

"As far as whether or not to quit acting, only you know that. But, I'll tell you this, young people hunt with a shotgun—it sprays everywhere, you're almost guaranteed a kill, even if it's a crappy one. But as you get older, if there's something you really want, put down your shot-gun and pick up a rifle. Rifle requires you to really be exact, it requires your time and focus, but if that's what you really want, it's worth it.

He then signed off by saying, "Hey, look at Jason Bateman, he went away for like a decade and now he's huge again."

Thanks, Harris, I don't know if I'll ever be able to truly articulate what this advice meant to me.

Harris was right, I was thirty-three and I didn't have to apologize for not being crystal clear on what the hell I was doing, it was okay to second-guess, to be unsure, to feel lost. I didn't have to walk around apologizing for the fact that I had once been so driven, so clear, and now, for maybe the first time, I was acting my age. Maybe who I was as a teenager and in my twenties didn't have to in-form who I was for the rest of my life. Maybe I could begin again.

When people over the years would ask, "Are you still acting?" I would respond in a nicely veiled, tightly jawed "Yes, I'm still acting" way. The tone was cordial but right underneath there was a whisper of "Don't ask me any more dumb questions." I was defensive, ultrasensitive, wounded, constantly trying to influence what other people thought. But after my conversation with Harris, I realized I could say something else, I could say, "No, I'm not acting anymore," and that was completely acceptable; in fact, it was better.

It wasn't an admission of defeat, it was an admission of closure. "Yes, that's something I did before, but I no longer do it." A lot of people work at coffee shops throughout their youth. I worked on TV, same thing. Instead of saying curtly that I was still acting and inviting whatever questions or thoughts the person had next, trying to navigate them to keep my ego intact, I politely cut them off at the pass, allowing them to wonder what I was doing with my life, or probably more accurately, stop thinking about me altogether.

The first time I let the words leave my mouth, "I'm not acting anymore," I felt empowered, untethered by this thing that I'd been married to my entire life. I didn't feel weak, I felt strong, having the courage to stare people and the world in the face and say, "I'm doing my best to figure out what's next and I'm not going to apologize for being relentlessly human."

Because no one leaves on their own accord, no one walks away from show business, especially once you've become a public person. Of course, there are some exceptions, but for most of us, there are two realities. The first, there's no suitable or realistic backup plan, so you milk every reality TV opportunity you can till Social Security kicks in. Second, you have to hide in plain sight because you'll always be the guy from that thing even if you're now also a successful real estate agent. Tough on the ol' ego.

I couldn't worry about that, that woman at that AA meeting was right. I kicked and screamed and did everything I could to avoid having to face this moment, acting wasn't part of who I was, it WAS who I was. It was woven through the deepest fibers of my being, it was my identity, and letting go of it was my greatest fear. But like most fears, once I took the cuffs off and invited its embrace, once I stared it down and said, "One of us is going to walk out of here alive," it faded to almost nothing. I felt free in a way I'd never felt before, not unlike when I gave up drinking, freedom through surrender.

My ego took its final breath and I felt it leave my body, at least temporarily. The ego has incredible recuperative powers, so it'd be insane to think it wouldn't come back in some form, but as it applied to this thing, this thing I'd fought for so long, it felt like I'd turned a corner.

I was making a living, I was a good dad, a good husband, and a good son. If I made it as an actor, it didn't matter anymore because I was already overpaid. I was one of the lucky ones whether I knew it or not, and for the first time I could accept how good my life had become without the caveat that if I only had X, I could be happy.

I was happy.

17

There Are No Experts of the Future

One last thing.

Remember that second part of Harris's advice? About picking up that metaphorical rifle and following what was really in my heart? Once I had stripped everything away, I was able to see clearly what I really wanted, what my truth was. I still loved acting and it wasn't because I wanted to impress you, or because I needed it to pay my rent. I didn't care anymore what you thought and my rent was paid for. I loved it for all the reasons I first did, sitting in that studio apartment at eight years old.

Over the past three years and even before that, I noticed I had become so bitter, so disillusioned, so frustrated by how my career was going that I had stopped enjoying acting altogether. I couldn't even watch movies anymore, it was just too painful. This coming from the same guy who would see movies twice or even three times in the theater, just to share his discovery with a friend who'd never heard of *The Diving Bell and the Butterfly* or *Rushmore* or *Lost in Translation*.

Driven by ego, my desire to please and impress had zapped the joy out of the thing I loved most. But now I no longer had anything attached to it, I could just be a viewer like I was when I was a kid. The weeks that followed my chat with Harris, I found myself back in my old routine of being transported by the movies I loved. I would watch *Searching for Bobby Fischer* or *Goodfellas* wishing I was in that park playing chess with Laurence Fishburne or maniacally laughing at some bar with De Niro. I would rewind scenes and study their performances, I got lost in the magic again.

And then I heard a voice. My father's voice.

Just kidding, that'd be ridiculous, I never even met the guy, how the fuck would I know what he sounded like? What I heard was a familiar voice that I've been hearing throughout most of my life. You know this voice, you HAVE this voice. It's the voice that tells you to go to the gym, not to eat trans fat, and call your mother. It's that inner governor, that idealized voice that wants the best for you. Now whether we listen to it or not is another story but the voice was telling me, on that day, to keep going. Just keep going.

What I realized, free from that old story in my head, was that if I still wanted to act, I could. I was making a living, spending time with my family, so if in the few hours a week I had to myself I wanted to spend it breaking down a scene, memorizing lines, and auditioning, well, that was my business. If eventually I had to miss one of Max's soccer games to audition for *CSI: Nebraska* that was one thing, but that wasn't the case, not yet.

So, I started again, but this time I did it for me. Not in the hopes I would have something exciting to talk about, or because I needed to prove to the world that I wasn't just another cautionary tale. I did it because I wanted to, because it pleased me, not because my ego ached for it. I could still get auditions, the same ones that the people who just moved to LA got, and that was good enough for me.

I've sat in black box theaters in Venice performing plays for an audience of ten, I've stood at the top of the Carpathian Mountains delivering dialogue in minus forty degree weather, I've cried to Ben Kingsley, been heckled onstage at twelve doing stand-up, performed for my phone in my car, and acted on my own TV show. It's just what I do; whatever the form, I do it.

I didn't tell anyone I was auditioning again. As far as everyone else was concerned, I'd still quit. I don't know, I just didn't want any questions such as "How'd your audition go?" or "Did ya hear anything?" or "They're going in a different direction? I'm so sorry." I didn't want any of it! This was between me and the universe, no one else.

I remember going to my first audition back, it was in a building I've been to perhaps a hundred times in my life. It's dead center in the middle of Los Angeles and houses about a dozen casting directors; they must figure since it's so central, it's an equally terrible commute for everyone. I have left that building more than a few times, throwing my script into the street, pulling my hair out, and looking for the closest place to buy cigarettes.

But this time I just walked in, sat down, and waited for my turn. I didn't get bogged down in the usual neurosis, plotting and planning how I was going to walk in there like the Second Coming, sizing up everyone in the waiting room and thinking, *Why's that guy here? I'm way better than that guy, ya know, if that's the direction they're going in, this whole thing is fucked, I should just leave, I should leave, right?* I was ready, I did the work, all I had to do was show them that. I remember sharing a smile at the end of the audition with the casting director, it was a thanks-for-doing-what-you-do-so-I-can-do-what-I-do type of smile. I hadn't had one of those ever.

Two weeks later, I booked the biggest job of my career since *The Wackness.* You saw that coming, right?

Look, as I write this, I've just finished shooting the first season of a new show I'm the lead of for Disney+. The show is slated to premiere in July of 2021, and this book is slated to be released in 2022. So by the time you read this, the show could very well be canceled, or the biggest thing in the world. Or given how the world works, *I could be canceled.* Or none of these, but here's the good news: it doesn't matter.

In times of frustration over the past decade, friends

in the business would say to me "Once you stop caring, that's when things will start happening, you just have to not care." I hated this advice because no matter how hard I tried to will myself into not caring, I ALWAYS CARED. This seemed impossible. The advice wasn't wrong, it was just the destination with no directions, like telling someone to "calm your mind" or "embrace your inner badass." It looks good on a T-shirt, but how the hell do you do it?

When I interviewed Neal Brennan, genius comedian and cocreator of *The Chappelle Show*, he said, "You'll probably get everything you ever wanted. It just won't be in the way you expected." He paused a moment and then added, "Actually, you'll probably get what you wanted, but by then you won't want it anymore."

Neal was right.

When I walked into that audition, I knew I was ready, I'd just spent three years pillorying myself in front of Sharon. I had fans at the network because I had worked with them before, and because of sobriety, I had learned how to be responsible, accountable, a good employee, and they knew that. They could count on me.

Here was the most important thing, I knew that when I was done, I got to go home to my wife and son, that no matter what the outcome, my life would only be slightly improved by it going my way. That was my ace in the hole, that was the energy I walked into that room with, I'd love to do the part but I don't need it. I have everything I need.

"A good life as the result of good living." I'll leave you with this final thought.

Safi Bahcall (Harvard physicist and cancer researcher) told the story of Dr. Judah Folkman on my podcast. In the early seventies, Judah, a young cancer surgeon, began noticing that the tumors he was removing from people's bodies were covered in blood vessels. He theorized that building a tumor was much like building a home; it required a foundation, and you had to lay pipes to bring in oxygen or nutrients and to take out waste. This mechanism is known as angiogenesis. What if we created a drug, he thought, that blocked those pipes, a drug that intercepted the signal from the tumor to the body telling it to build more foundation.

At this time, the primary treatment for cancer was either radiation (burn it) or chemotherapy (poison it). He was met with incredible resistance. He was called crazy, received countless rejection letters, and eventually was asked to either stop his research or resign his position at his hospital because he was thought to be simply wasting time. He resigned and, for thirty years, continued his research.

In 2003, at a major cancer research conference in Chicago, a doctor gave a presentation describing the results of one of the largest trials ever done in colon cancer, evaluating a drug based on Judah's ideas. He said, "Here are the results: patients who received Judah's drug, lived longer than anyone has ever lived before with metastatic colon cancer." Standing ovation, the place erupted, one of the speakers onstage said, "If only Dr. Folkman were alive to see this moment."

Judah was actually in the audience, but he simply turned to a colleague and smiled.

He had transformed the world of cancer treatment, and today there's an entirely new class of antiangiogenic drugs that came directly from Judah's lab. Oh, and these treatments led to a company called Celgene, which recently sold for one hundred billion dollars. Safi wound up working with Judah in the early 2000s and asked him, "How did you persist? Through years, through all these ups and downs and people telling you every day that this will never work?"

Dr. Folkman responded, "Safi, there are no experts of the future."

Conclusion
Happy People Are (Still) Annoying

So here we are at the end of the book. Did you really read this whole thing? I have my doubts. You're a skimmer, aren't you? A couple of pages from each chapter? Be honest. The truth is, same. If this weren't my book I'm not sure I would've read the whole thing; my copy editor could've very well replaced pages 96 through 111 with his own manifesto and in most cases I'd never know it.

I remember early on in getting sober, I was being petulant about the efficacy of certain meetings, feeling as though I wasn't hearing a lot during my one-hour deluge into group spirituality that resonated. Bits and pieces for sure but maybe not like a big ol' helping of breakthrough. It was then when a friend told me, "That's because the entire meeting isn't for you. It's for the group. If you take 5 percent away from this meeting, then that's great because the other 95 percent is for everyone else. They need to identify with something as well."

So, if you magically turned to page one, took something away from it, and then promptly left this book inside whatever godforsaken coffee shop you found it in, excellent. And if you had to suffer through every page to discover that seed of insight that will prove beneficial in your life, then I'm sorry, but also excellent. And if by some miracle you made it through this book enjoying every page, I'd say thank you for reading my book, Mom, and also, can you please make Rice Krispies Treats more often because even as a man in my thirties, they still bring me absurd amounts of comfort.

God, I want to wrap this thing up for you in the most psychically reassuring bow right now. I'd love to send you off into the world with some new insight, some sense of purpose, that feeling of "Look out, world, not only do I READ BOOKS but also I WORK on myself!"

I guess it would behoove us to speak about happiness one last time, what I think of it now as opposed to when we started. Here's what I know. Happiness is the name of a state of being associated with a number of fleeting feelings that are pleasurable, temporary, and brief. Happy is like the weather, unapologetically ever changing. I used to think happiness was a destination, a byzantine place that required a mysterious toll you had to pay over and over again to finally be allowed admittance.

Here's what I think of it now: it's overrated. The thirteenth-century Persian poet Rumi said, "We seek neither to despair, nor rejoice." I couldn't have said it better myself, but I'll try. What I think Rumi meant is, life is ineffable. It's too weird and complex to reduce down to a single word such as happy. Life is relentless, it's very much in session, and it's throwing everything it's got at us at all times. So congratulations, you get to feel the full spectrum of human emotions life has to offer, and if you've done the work, if you've participated in life and not run from it, then you're equipped to do it.

"Too much sunshine brings about a desert," a friend once told me. The universe demands balance, I guess the same could be said about life. As sure as the tough times are coming, the good times are coming too. Joy will come as quickly and as strongly as sadness will and the cycle will repeat in a beautifully fucked-up ballet of ups and downs till the sun eats the earth. But I now know one thing for sure:

The hard times are here to teach us, and the good times are to remind us what we're fighting for.

Here's the last thing I'll say: follow me on Instagram. No. Here's the last thing I'll say: it wasn't supposed to happen for me like this. I've sat with my shrink during moments of immense gratitude high off of something as innocuous as watching my son roll around on a gymnasium floor for an hour and said, "I just can't believe this is my life. It wasn't supposed to happen like this."

It was then when he interrupted and said, "Stop saying

that. It was supposed to happen for you. You faced immense challenge, nothing was given to you, you had to face your demons at every turn, and you did it. You deserve this life you've built; I've watched you build it."

Maybe, and I can appreciate that. I can also honor that a clinician of his caliber, one who has been able to stand me as a client for more than fifteen years, is probably aware of certain subtleties I am not. I'm sure of it. I mean, at this point, I've paid him the equivalent of what would be the value of a pretty loaded midsize sedan, so I feel that I have to agree with him.

Just know I almost gave up a thousand times. Just know that despite how good my life is, when faced with adversity, my mind still romanticizes getting a bunch of drugs and some White Castle hamburgers and seeing what happens. Just know that I still don't really feel comfortable at parties. Just know that you can do whatever I did but better, and that when you do, I'll expect you to write the book for the next round of people like us.

Okay, that's it.

Acknowledgments

I want to thank Ryan Holiday, without whom this book would suck. I didn't know when I met you fifteen years ago that you would become one of the most prolific writers of our time. Thank you for guiding me through this process, and being so generous with your talent. You embody everything you write about and I feel lucky to call you a friend.

Sydney Rogers, you're a dream. From our first call to the final edit, I felt a special bond with you right away and that has not changed. You are everything I could've asked for in an editor, a gentle support rooting me on the entire way, with an insanely high level of skill to help make the bad good and the good great. Thank you one million times.

Albert Lee, thank you for being my hype man when this book was nothing more than an idea, and for assuring me that I had something to write about. Pilar Queen, thank you for your support and insight throughout this process, you're an expert at what you do and this book is so much better for it. And thank you for the title.

David Buchatler, thank you for convincing me to not only write a book, but for getting Albert to beat down my door until I did. This entire process started with you and I'm so grateful.

Dan Strachman. When I was eight years old, my mom walked me into the Jewish Big Brother's office to meet Dan, who was a twenty-four-year-old finance guy looking to do some good. From that moment on Dan has been my Big Brother, and while we're not bonded by blood, we're connected by twenty-seven years of being a part of each other's lives. Dan gave me the ultimate gift, his time, and the only reason I don't talk about him more in the book is because our relationship has been so unwaveringly good that there's no drama to it. He's also an accomplished author and was kind enough to give me notes not just on this book but on everything I write. Dan, you're my family, thank you for everything.

Sam Maydew, Shani Rosenzweig, and Jacob Fenton, what a team. Thank you for standing by me through all the ups and downs. Multidecade relationships are rare in show business but so are the three of you. You guys believed in me even when I started to lose faith, and you weren't afraid to hurt my feelings when you knew it would do me the most good.

Thank you most of all to my family. Barbara Peck, Paige Peck, Max Peck, and the O'Briens. Life is sweetest when I'm with you.

About Josh Peck

Josh Peck is an actor, comedian, and I guess an author now. Podcasts, social media, speaking engagements blah blah blah.